1971

Donnac

University of St. Francis
GEN 110 D578
Dilley
Metaphysics and religious lang

W9-ADJ-376

Metaphysics and Religious Language

Metaphysics and
Religious Language

FRANK B. DILLEY

COLUMBIA UNIVERSITY PRESS

New York and London 1964

LIBRARY
College of St. Francis
JOLIET, ILL.

Frank B. Dilley is a member of the Department of
Philosophy at Millikin University, Decatur, Illinois.

Copyright © 1964 Columbia University Press
Library of Congress Catalog Card Number: 64-7766
Manufactured in the United States of America

110
D578

To Leonard Pinsky and Edmond Cherbonnier
who made me think
and to Paul Tillich and Daniel Day Williams
who helped me understand

59290

Contents

Metaphysics and Religious Language

Introduction

———⬥———

Immanuel Kant started something which he did not finish, the "Copernican revolution" in philosophy which turned philosophical scrutiny upon the knower rather than the known. Awakened from his "dogmatic slumber" by David Hume, Kant attempted to find philosophical security in conceptual processes, asserting that there are certain inevitable categories of thinking which cannot be doubted because they are the very categories through which thinking takes place. But Kant did not know, nor did any of his generation know, the degree to which the categories Kant defended were relative to his time and place.

While there are those who would still defend those categories, it has become possible to doubt them in a way which Kant did not anticipate. The development of non-Euclidean geometries and of non-Aristotelian logics, the discovery of relativism in all its varieties, and the awareness that there are whole cultures and whole language systems which do not structure reality in the traditional western European way have caused recent philosophy to turn from Kant's certainties. The certainty about the external world which Kant dissolved has been followed by a dissolving of his certainty about the conceptual world.

Characteristic of recent thought has been a widespread awareness of the conditioned or relative character of knowledge, and an extensive literature on philosophical method, on symbolic activity, and on the nature of religious truth has arisen in response to this awareness. Susanne Langer, in *Philosophy in a New Key,* noted that in the twenty years prior to 1939 there were sixteen major philosophical works related to semantics alone, and her list was not exhaustive; nor did it include the many articles and chapters of books on that subject, nor any of the related inquiries that have occupied philosophical attention of late.

The purpose of the present writing is to make use of ideas presented by many such studies to show their implications for understanding the nature of metaphysical thinking. An attempt has been made to gather and coordinate from a variety of sources a general theory of metaphysics and of symbolism which states in comprehensive fashion the general consensus which has emerged in recent times.

Specifically, an attempt is made to show that, whether one is interested in discussing the nature of philosophical method, theories of symbols and symbol interpretation, or theories of revelation, the same ideas and problems inevitably arise. Traditional rules have been called radically into question and for good reason. The various schools of philosophers find themselves in disagreement not only as to logical rules but also as to what even the basic facts really are. Inquiries into the "logics" of various languages, analyses of the presuppositions and assumptions of metaphysical systems, the elaboration of the relativistic implications of historical and cultural studies and of studies in physics and psychology, all these have been prominent features of contemporary philosophical discussion.

The major concern in this writing is with what is often called meta-metaphysics, and not with the advocacy of any particular metaphysical view. The discussion of this issue is not phrased in "the linguistic idiom" for the most part; hence instead of "meta-metaphysics" the term "theory of metaphysics" has been used.

By "metaphysics" is meant the philosophical discipline concerned with discovering the ideas which are indispensable to the analysis of everything that happens, the discipline concerned with describing the nature of things, to use two of Alfred North White-head's descriptions. It is distinguished from science in being concerned with the whole of reality, not selected aspects, and therefore its theories are world theories, not theories limited to realities of special kinds as are the sciences and other specialized disciplines.

It is distinguished from religion in that religion is concerned with human attitudes toward what is taken to be ultimate, and what can be done to foster and conserve these attitudes. Religions have metaphysical implications because they imply that certain things are true about this world, but they are not religious in virtue of that. Metaphysical theories state ideas as to what is really ultimate, but they are not metaphysical in virtue of that. The religious function of propositions is expressive and hortatory and the metaphysical function is cognitive.

A usage has been adopted which perhaps blurs this distinction, but it has been adopted because it is so frequently used in the literature on this subject. The claim is made that metaphysical descriptions arise out of basic assumptions or perspectives, and the word "faith" is used to describe the attitude taken toward these perspectives or assumptions. It cannot be said that basic assumptions are justified in terms of reason, since what seems reasonable is a function of those assumptions. Nor can it be said that they are justified in terms of fact, since what is seen as factual is a function of those assumptions. It is not argument of any sort that justifies the assumptions because argument presupposes them, and the conclusions of argument are shaped by them.

The term "faith" has been employed to describe the attitude taken toward such assumptions. In this sense "faith" is defined as an attitude of trust or orientation taken toward that which seems undeniable up to now, yet cannot be rationally proved because it stands prior to proof. Santayana had this sort of thing in mind in speaking of "animal faith," although other philosophers prefer to use more neutral words such as "intuition." The word "faith" is also used, by extension, to refer to the basic assumptions themselves.

A metaphysical system could thus be described as a reasoned and elaborated faith, the system presenting an attempt to organize reality in terms consistent with that faith, perhaps in order to test its adequacy as a starting point for metaphysics. Faiths, in this sense, are not inflexible. The original insight might very well be refined in the course of elaboration and extension, and sometimes there are radical changes which take place.

Two statements in anticipation of objections seem to be in order. It is often pointed out, in an effort to discredit theories such as the ones presented herein, that, if true, these theories leave the philosopher with no bedrock certainties. It would be a dangerous procedure to reject these theories on this ground. Arguments must be fought with arguments, not with wishes. The mere fact that it might be desirable to have more certainty than these theories leave does not in any way establish the *right* to believe that this certainty is possible. The theories presented here are defended because the analyses lead to them, although one cannot rule out the possibility that the author takes secret joy in being insecure.

Secondly, it is sometimes said that such theories as these are self-contradictory because they claim that it can be known with certainty that nothing can be known. In answer to this charge it should be pointed out that the theories do not say this. What is claimed is not that it can be proved that no one knows anything, since it may be that many of the things that philosophers think that they know are actually true. What these theories state is merely that it is impossible to know for certain which statements are true and which are false. The theories suggested in this book do not contend that absolute skepticism should be followed, merely that absolute certainty cannot be established.

The thesis that the nature of metaphysical thinking is best described in terms of a "root-metaphor" or "confessionalist" or "tentative hypothesis" theory of metaphysics is presented at length and defended. Effort is made to detail the consequences of such a theory for problems of metaphysical method and of symbology. That all metaphysical thinking is shaped not only by what is "out there" but also by antecedent metaphysical assumptions which determine in part how reality is seen, what methods are thought to yield cognitive results, and what kinds of symbols and modes of symbolic reference are deemed necessary has important consequences. What seems to be true is in part conditioned by the perspective through which things are viewed.

Similarly, what cognitive methods are regarded as informative and what types of symbols and modes of symbolic reference are deemed to be necessary are also conditioned by perspective. The adoption of a criterion of truth, or of factuality, assumes the validity of the kind of metaphysic which is the legitimate parent of such a criterion, and can be known to be valid only if the adequacy of the parent system can be established. To assert the sufficiency of a particular cognitive method is at the same time to assert or "confess" the adequacy of some particular metaphysic, as is also the case with the assertion of a particular view of the facts.

Peculiar problems raised traditionally by theism, having to do with peculiarities of language, of cognitive method, and of modes of symbolic reference, are discussed. Some aspects of recent discussion concerning theism and the verification principle are presented, and the unverifiability of theism *in these terms* is accepted without alarm. The attempt to derive religious language from authority is presented and rejected, and it is argued that the "tentative hypothesis" theory of metaphysics provides a more adequate analysis of the way in which theistic discussion is actually carried on, however some theologians may choose to describe their activities themselves.

A chapter on symbols develops the thesis that questions about the adequacy of special terms or of special modes of symbolic reference are basically metaphysical questions, undecidable except as metaphysical questions are decided because of the way in which particular symbologies are related to particular metaphysical descriptions.

Some consequences for the problem of establishing the adequacy of metaphysical systems are detailed. Some ways to establish the existence of God are examined, and an attempt is made to bring all of the legitimate types of proof into harmony with the "root-metaphor" theory of metaphysics.

The attempt is not to defend any particular metaphysic, but only to present and defend a particular theory of the nature of metaphysics, to delineate the kinds of problems which must be discussed and the kinds of appeals which must be made in establishing the validity of particular metaphysical descriptions. The investigation is merely a prolegomenon to the more crucial tasks of creating and defending actual metaphysical descriptions, and of ascertaining what religious symbols are the cognitively adequate ones.

I. The Nature of
Philosophical Disagreement

Philosophers *do* agree about many things not only in using a common language but also in acknowledging, at least provisionally, that there seems to be a world of "plain facts" known in much the same way to everyone and relatively independent of one's philosophical commitments. Philosophical disputes do not usually occur over whether or not there *seems* to be such a thing as the thermos bottle on my desk, but philosophers do disagree as to what, if anything, is the reality underlying the appearance that is called the thermos bottle.[1]

At this level many differing answers are furnished by the varying philosophical traditions. The competing schools offer their own accounts of what the basic realities are, presenting their own distinctive visions of the *real* facts. A philosophical position does not, then, present a common-sense view of the "plain facts," which competes against opposed presentations of the "plain facts," for a philosophy offers a critical account of the facts rather than the plain ones; it presents a view as to what the *real* facts are. Tennyson holds that out of the simplest flower in the crannied wall one can learn what God and man are; more "common-sense" philosophers attempt to show that the real facts are more or less the plain ones; and mystical and/or solipsistic philosophers undertake to make the plain facts "softly and silently vanish away and never be met with again."

Thus, although philosophers agree on one level, speaking

about the world of ordinary experience in similar ways, they disagree markedly on the deeper level, and the student of philosophy is confronted by a considerable number of competing views as to how the world *really* goes. John Laird, describing the recent philosophical world, states this situation as follows:

"Back to Kant," "Back to Hume," "Back to Locke," "Back to St. Thomas," "Back to Plato." All these things are said to-day, in all seriousness, by very eminent people—sometimes, indeed, by the same people.

. . . The philosophical past has not been buried, and there is no general agreement, I think, to the effect that any of the larger metaphysical ideas of the past should now be regarded as unhappy ghosts. There are outcries, no doubt, against substance; but many competent philosophers are still substantialists. The recent confident revolt against a causality that is something more than uniform sequence has already subsided in many quarters. Dualism, representationism and other such theories, discarded by some, have been rescued by others. To-day there are would-be solipsists, would-be pan-sensualists, would-be neo-Protagoreans, would-be apostles of common sense. What was supposed to be Kant's greatest discovery, the discovery, namely of synthetic judgments *a priori,* is repudiated in set terms by an important philosophical school. In short many things commonly regarded as philosophical crudities or absurdities are still maintained by competent people; and other competent people are eager to take the risk of setting back the clock.

With greater resources for illuminating, man should become less afraid of the twilight. Yet his eyes are but human, and time itself will not permanently improve them.[2]

The question that arises is why this is so, why it is that "greater resources for illuminating" do not permanently improve man's philosophical eyes. The answer lies in the kind of thinking that philosophizing basically is. The fundamental task of this inquiry is to lay bare the structure of philosophical thinking and system building in such a way as to show why philosophers disagree, why philosophy is pluralistic, why the same basic problems that divided Greek minds into competing schools continue to divide moderns from each other. The problems seem inescapable and unsolvable, hence their persistence.

Occasionally, however, one finds analyses of basic philosophical disagreement which badly oversimplify both disagreements and prospects for resolution of disagreements. Hence it is useful at this point to sketch in an introductory fashion several theories as to why philosophers disagree, a sketch followed by a brief presentation of the views on the nature of philosophical thinking which are defended throughout this inquiry.

Some Inadequate Theories

Many answers to the question as to why philosophers disagree require the supposition that disagreements are merely apparent, not real, or else that the disagreement is over something that can be cleared up rather easily. Such answers are confronted by the obvious difficulty that philosophers do not seem to be the sort of people who are easily duped on philosophical matters. Some variations on these two themes follow.

1. Sometimes it is held that basic disputes arise from a confusion of linguistic difficulties with real ones. The problem of whether or not a sound is made by a tree crashing in a forest where there is no one to hear is a case in point. Linguistic analysis solves this problem, and some philosophers hope that such analysis will solve all others. It is sometimes claimed, also, that there is some one perennial philosophy which seems to appear in many forms owing to the use of different myths and images, but which is *really* the same, so that a basic unity of viewpoint underlies the apparent diversity of philosophical

thought. A number of philosophers make this claim, offering what are apparently different philosophies as the perennial one.

Were this the case, greater resources for illuminating, better knowledge of variations in cultures and languages, ought to lead to the dissolution of basic problems, but the results are often quite the opposite. Philosophical disputes seldom vanish because of increased illumination. One would expect, were this claim true, that all basic disagreements would have disappeared long ago as it became increasingly clear that differences were purely verbal. Contrariwise, the continued presence of basic disputes, their resistance to extinction, itself shows that translation is not the answer. Philosophers persist in thinking that they really disagree, even after having read the books which purport to show that they do not.

2. It is sometimes suggested that apparently differing views can be shown to be really in agreement through the creation of some synthesis. Higher truth may perhaps be found by adding all the partial truths together, as is the case with the blind men and the elephant. Or, perhaps, the truth is to be found through perceiving the dialectical pattern which unites, preserves, and transcends the partial truths, as Hegel suggested.

But here, too, the presence of competing syntheses and the resistance of philosophers to being swallowed up into someone else's system constitute a difficulty. There is a sense in which every philosophical system offers itself as the synthesis, since every system provides a place for rejected alternatives, either by incorporation or by exclusion. Likewise the continued dispute as to which synthesis to use indicates resistance on all sides to everyone else's candidate. Had this issue been settled, had all views been actually reconciled, then the disputes would not persist. Conversely, the persistence of disputes indicates the failure of any synthesis to carry the day. Everyone expects everyone else to fold his tent and silently steal away, and no one prepares to fold his own.

3. Often it is suggested that basic philosophical disagreements result from mistakes, simple factual or logical errors. Such an analysis is encountered with disturbing frequency as one reads "refutations" of this or that position. One philosopher writes a refutation of idealism, another of realism, and Dr. Johnson thought he disposed of Berkeley by merely kicking a stone! Some philosophers are forever refuting theism by "showing" that the arguments for the existence of God are vitiated by logical improprieties; others refute atheism by "showing" that to trust reason or to act ethically is to presuppose the existence of God. Thus philosophers imply that their adversaries are guilty of sheer error, of failure to notice some fact or of failure to observe some logical rule.

There are at least two difficulties with such analyses. The first is that philosophers have good reasons for "failing to notice" the alleged facts or rules. Philosophers refuse to admit that they have made mistakes despite the best efforts of others to prove that they have. Secondly, the disputes in question are often disputes *over* the facts and the logical rules. One cannot accuse an opponent of failing to notice a fact or rule when he knows very well what it is and has deliberately rejected its decisiveness. Berkeley knew very well that stones could be kicked and was, in fact, offering a philosophical view which *denied* that Dr. Johnson's interpretation of stone kicking was adequate. The "plain facts" were known; the real facts were in dispute.

Basic philosophical disputes, in short, are not always disputes *within* some commonly accepted view as to what facts and logic are; they are often disputes as to what the facts are and as to which logical rules are useful in philosophizing.

4. Sometimes, especially of late, it is claimed that philosophers do not really disagree because they are not saying anything. It is sometimes claimed that metaphysical "statements" are only pseudo-assertions, not the sort of thing about which one can really agree or disagree. Rudolf Carnap, for example, has claimed that metaphysical propositions are not assertions but expressions. Likening them to lyric poetry, he asserts that their function is to express "permanent emotional and volitional dispositions." [3] Since such propositions do not assert anything, that is, since they do not offer anything in the way of a factual or logical claim, it is not proper to speak of them as conflicting at all. Once such pseudo-propositions have been relegated to the realm of poetry, the field of truth is then left to the scientists, who are not, Carnap seems to presume, plagued by basic disputes. Disagreements disappear, scientists provide our knowledge of the world, metaphysicians express their feelings about the world but do not talk about it, and the problem is solved.

In anticipation of the results of a presentation and critique of this point of view, two obvious difficulties can be seen. First, such a view implies that no philosopher prior to the twentieth century really knew what he was talking about much of the time. He *thought* that he was talking about reality but now he is known to have been talking merely about his psychic states. Secondly, such an analysis proceeds on the supposition that there are no real metaphysical disputes about the adequacy of radical empiricism as a final criterion of truth. However, it is precisely this question that is at issue in many disputes.

Such a view avoids some of the oversimplifications already discussed. While it is difficult to think that basic disagreements arise from logical and/or observational errors, it is plausible, in this age of psychoanalysis, to suppose that disagreements might reflect nonrational factors. Morris Lazerowitz, more than any other contemporary, has defended the theory and it is to a presentation and critique of his claims that the discussion now turns.

A Psychoanalytic Explanation

Lazerowitz, dismissing attempts to explain metaphysical disputes in terms of simple error as obviously inadequate once the competence of philosophers is granted, draws the following conclusion: "When continued confrontation with plain fact does not make philosophers give up their theory, it is safest to proceed on the assumption, not that their intelligence is weak, but that somehow the facts do not count against the theory." [4] Instead of interpreting this to mean that the metaphysicians are thereby claiming that "plain fact" is not *real* fact, Lazerowitz concludes that philosophers are not concerned with the facts at all; instead they are building verbal fantasies. "Like a dream, a metaphysical theory is a production of the unconscious" (SM, 26). The function of metaphysical theories is to satisfy wishes and fears in the substratum of our minds; thus "the metaphysician can with hardly any exaggeration be said to use his statement *solely* to express unconscious material" (SM, 78). Elsewhere he speaks of philosophical theories as "nothing more than subtle, highly intellectualized ways of expressing and satisfying needs of the 'twilight' (and darker) parts of our minds," giving expression *only* to "unconscious fantasies." [5] For example, he claims the real meaning of the words "nothing ever changes" is that "no changes which would create anxiety in me are real" (SM, 70). Thus the speaker of these words refers not to external fact but to his inner needs.

It is apparent that Lazerowitz means this analysis to apply to all disputes about propositions which are "not resolvable by scientific means of any sort" (SM, 25). He claims that a "prop-

osition is not about reality, about the nature of things," if it
has no refutation in terms of some actual or imaginable series
of sense observations (SM, 61). In discussing a metaphysical
dispute concerning tables he points out that the matter in question is not subject to "resolution by any sort of examination
of things and that it is not, therefore, about their nature"
(PSP, 140).

Seemingly of the opinion that all the proper philosophical
disputes have been solved in favor of the view that the "plain
facts" are the real facts, he claims that "all the facts, material
or linguistic, that are relevant to the solution of the problem
are perfectly well known by the metaphysicians who take part
in the dispute. There is no question of a super fact-finder
breaking the deadlock. This makes it clear that the disagreement is not factual, not about what is or is not the case"
(SM, 64).

The suggestion that philosophical disputes might persist because of the "complexity and difficulty of the problems dealt
with" he dismisses by saying merely that this is not an "im-
pressive possibility" and that it "need not detain us" (SM, 24);
accordingly, he never discusses it. Presumably, then, his claim
is that the basic facts are the real facts, that science is the obvious arbiter of what is and is not the case, and that one must
turn to psychoanalysis in order to understand what it is that
metaphysicians are doing since their views do not square with
"the facts."

The suggestion is not utterly implausible, and is surely worthy
of careful consideration, both because Lazerowitz is a very
competent philosopher and because his views can receive considerable psychoanalytic support. The noncognitive functions
of "reason" are too well known to require comment.

However, the persistence of metaphysics and its unsolved disputes requires another sort of analysis, one which recognizes that a philosopher can be talking about the facts yet at the same time be rejecting the ultimacy of the plain facts. The key difficulty with Lazerowitz is, as Charles Frankel has observed, his unwarranted "sense of assurance that some truths in philosophy are so clear that one must go to pathology to explain why otherwise intelligent men do not see them" (PSP, 327).

Lazerowitz grossly oversimplifies the philosophical task, as the foregoing citations of his views have indicated. It is not unquestionably clear that the "plain facts" are the full facts, yet he does not seem ever to entertain the idea that sane men might dispute this claim. In this regard, what Lazerowitz does not discuss is fully as illuminating of his position as the passages to which reference has been made. Already noted has been his dismissal of the possibility that complexity might be a factor in basic philosophical disagreement. Nowhere does he indicate that there might be *legitimate* discussion as to whether the plain facts are really the full facts. It is never suggested that rival metaphysicians might possibly be challenging his view that the plain facts are the real facts. Nowhere is there any indication that philosophers might deliberately reject the metaphysical adequacy of the "plain facts." To speak of them as though they were being deceived by their words, as though *they had meant to be talking about the plain facts* but had somehow failed, is to misrepresent these philosophers. In short, Lazerowitz supposes that when a person contradicts "plain fact" he needs to be understood psychoanalytically, whereas what is the case is that such a person is deliberately rejecting the adequacy of the plain facts for philosophy.

In short, Lazerowitz proposes his views as a hypothesis regarding what is taking place when metaphysicians utter the expressions that they do. His hypothesis is not disprovable, but it is not provable either. It might be that the philosophers in question *really* agree as to all the facts, but they do not seem to, and they offer good reasons for not doing so, reasons which Lazerowitz either rejects or ignores.

The theory is not provable because even if one were able to show that there is always a relation between metaphysical belief and the unconscious, and even if one were able to demonstrate that *some* metaphysical theories are mere verbal fantasies, one could not even hope to be able to prove that *all* metaphysical utterances could be exhaustively analyzed in such terms. The question of the truth or falsity of the theories cannot be settled in these terms, for as someone has observed, "We may have come to believe that two times two equals four, because mothers give smiles and candy when we first recite the multiplication table, or because our minds have a tendency to certain rhythmic groupings. And yet two times two may really equal four." [6] Philosophical assertions, likewise, may serve unconscious needs and at the same time be true.

Metaphysical descriptions pretend at least to be versions of the *real* facts and often involve claims that the "plain facts" are in need of metaphysical criticism. Lazerowitz's claim is that the plain facts as analyzed by science are the real facts, whereas other metaphysicians claim that some other accounts of the facts are more adequate. It is not a case of admitted agreement on basic issues plus different wishes and unconscious strivings, as Lazerowitz maintains, but real disagreement on basic issues.

Why Philosophers Disagree

The question must now be faced: Why *do* philosophers disagree, not only with each other but often with the so-called plain facts of science and of common-sense experience? There are at least four factors, all of which have some connection with the *complexity* of reality and of metaphysical thinking, that contribute to persistent disagreement among metaphysicians.

Briefly, the four factors are: (a) the numerous levels and types of experiences for which cognitive claims can be made, (b) the numerous structures within each level that may be regarded as the basic keys or clues to metaphysical relationships, (c) the conditioned and to some extent self-conditioning character of metaphysical thinking, conceiving, perceiving, etc., and (d) the basic rootage of metaphysics in something akin to what religion has called "faith." Brief descriptions of each type of factor will follow, after one rather obvious observation.

Reality, prima facie, is complex. Certainly philosophers have always held that it is, that men are faced by a "buzzing, blooming confusion," in the midst of which they attempt to create or to discover some order or pattern. Philosophical theories, like other theories, offer handles by which reality can be grasped, conceptual schema in terms of which the whole of reality can be understood. Out of the welter of data, certain key relations and structures are chosen by competing theorists as *the* ones which seem to be the really significant ones. A philosophical theory, therefore, is a selection from a wider mass, a selection of those elements which seem to be essential for a metaphysical understanding of reality.

A. There are many levels or areas of human experience, each of which might prove to give primary access to the nature of the real. Perhaps scientific data, perhaps data from the realm of aesthetics or morals, perhaps data such as experiences of transcendent unity, perhaps "intuitions of being and intelligibility," perhaps experiences of order or experiences of chance and disorder are the basic data for metaphysics. Positivists tend toward sense data as the key realm of experience; classical philosophers tend to stress depths of being or experiences of transcendence; mystics tend to find only the realm of mystic awareness to be informative, and so on. There are quite clearly many types and levels of experience for which cognitive claims have been advanced, and, because this is so, there arise questions as to which type or types are cognitively significant. Some disagreement, then, is constituted by disputes as to which level or levels of experience are most significant.

B. Within each particular level or area of human experience, competing concepts or categories may be supported as the key ones. Stephen Pepper suggests, in expounding his "root-metaphor" theory of metaphysics, that there are a number of different categories that have actually proved to be very adequate and which recur frequently through the ages: similarity, form and matter, push and pull, organic whole, and temporal process (generating immanent realism, transcendent realism, mechanism, idealism, and contextualism respectively) are those he prefers, but he admits that there are also two other widely employed root metaphors which define the two great forms of religious tradition, animism and mysticism. His claim is that each of the first five metaphors, in elaborated form, is sufficiently wide in scope to have the status of a world hypothesis. Mysticism and animism fail to be comprehensive enough in his judgment. Each hypothesis illuminates reality in a unique, important, and irreplaceable way, hence each must be utilized. Each also has difficulties which prevent it from ever becoming a wholly adequate theory. Thus he advocates retaining all five metaphors, holding that each is irreplaceable and that no synthesis is possible, a conclusion which ought to be debated.[7]

The point is that there are a number of competing views of what the facts really are, each defended by well-trained philosophers who seem to be in possession of their faculties, each offering a particular set of categories and relationships as the most adequate key to the nature of things. Perhaps it can be said, as Lazerowitz suggests, that all these competing philosophers really "know" what the plain facts are, but it cannot be said that all these philosophers really agree with his claim that the criticized facts, the real facts, are the same as the plain ones, for each offers a different critical account of them. Philosophers all "know," loosely, what actions would ordinarily be called "voluntary," but they would at the same time disagree as to what these "voluntary" actions *really* are. A mechanist would argue that they are *really* involuntary or else redefine the normal meaning of "voluntary," whereas a voluntarist would defend some sort of faculty of, or capacity for, free will.

C. Further complicating metaphysical discussion is the problem of philosophical relativity, which affects the thinking process itself. Philosophers would disagree even if the two sources of disagreement previously mentioned did not affect them. Relativity can be overstated and must be balanced by other considerations; however, the claim that thinking processes and perceptual processes are conditioned, relative in part to environmental, social, and personal factors, is undoubtedly a true one. The evidence for some degree of philosophical relativity is overwhelming, and the question now is merely that of the extent of this relativity and whether or not some particular set of concepts can be defended as true despite cultural relativism.

For example, comparative linguistics has indicated that the assumption that all men are really the same, that they think alike and structure reality alike, is at best dubious. Linguistic structures differ not only from culture to culture but also from age to age. Symbolic forms, perceptual forms, grammatical forms, the sorts of structure that are taken to be basic, the realms of human experience that are taken to be most informative about the nature of things, laws of thinking that are employed, rules of evidence—all these things, and many more, are to some degree relative to particular cultures, ages, and interests, as well as to one's own metaphysical position. Many excellent authorities will be mustered in support of this claim; at this point only one statement is offered. Benjamin Whorf has made the following claim, arising out of his studies of primitive cultures: "All observers are not led by the same physical evidence to the same picture of the universe, unless their linguistic backgrounds are similar, or can in some way be calibrated." [8] He further observes that we can no longer claim that a few recent Indo-European dialects and the thought processes that go with them are the only possible patterns for thought. We know that they are *not* the only patterns, and recent critical inquiry, both scientific and philosophical, has caused many to suspect that these patterns are in basic respects misleading. One thinks of Russell's attack on subject-predicate language, Whitehead's criticism of simple location, the development of symbolic logic, philosophies of process, and so on.

Also, as Lazerowitz is undoubtedly correct in pointing out, metaphysical descriptions are related to factors of psychological conditioning, perceptual and conceptual, conscious and unconscious, character structure, unconscious needs, habits of perception and conception, even bodily dispositions, as simple introspection sometimes shows.

The claim that is being made here is not that all metaphysical positions are equally good, nor is it that all metaphysical positions are inevitably misled by relativizing influences. It is not at all clear that such influences necessarily falsify. The claim is merely that many influences inevitably affect men's thought. An adequate grammar would influence one's thinking just as much as an inadequate one; thus one can be guided for good or for ill.

Likewise with truth criteria, the scientific and religious ideas of one's age, and so on, the influence *can* lead to truth. It is a logical mistake to equate relativism and skepticism or subjectivism and there is nothing in any of the ideas defended in this book which is incompatible with the claim that there is objective truth or with claims to have that truth. Difficulty is raised not for claims to have truth but merely for claims to be able to *prove* in any logically conclusive way that one has it. That no one has devised such a proof is shown by the existence of the kind of basic metaphysical disagreement being discussed as well as by the analyses of metaphysical thinking which appear here and which will be presented more fully in subsequent chapters.

D. One further and more controversial factor making for metaphysical diversity must be introduced, and that is that metaphysical positions are ultimately built upon something akin to what theologians call faith. This is meant in at least two senses.

1. Metaphysical descriptions are elaborated judgments as to what ultimately is cognitively revealing, judgments as to what ultimately is really real. Such basic judgments constitute the fundamental framework to which all else is fit, influencing what one takes to be fact, one's methods and criteria, even one's perception of the world. Various philosophers *do* seem to see things differently and this seeing-things-differently, even after long periods of critical reflection, seems to be a function of different basic judgments as to what is informative about reality. An empiricist builds upon the judgment of the sufficiency of sense data, whereas there are other metaphysicians who depend upon so-called depth experiences that transcend ordinary sense data, and yet others who base their views upon private mystical experiences available only to a few or on religious experiences which are taken to be communications from a Divine Being.

2. There is another sense of the word "faith" which must also

be considered, both because there are a number of thinkers who claim to base their metaphysical insights on "faith" in this second sense, and because it is certainly a logical possibility that ultimate metaphysical insight may thus be derived, whether one believes that it actually is derived this way or not. Some metaphysicians, especially in modern Protestant circles but not exclusively there, have claimed that knowledge of ultimate reality, and hence full knowledge of every reality, has a basis which is neither perceptual nor rational in the ordinary senses of those words. God can be known only through His revelation of Himself, the receiving and accepting of which is called faith. God's existence cannot be demonstrated by means of some pure rational faculty, nor can He be directly experienced, nor can His existence be verified or falsified in terms of appeals to any particular experiences. Such a God, they claim, can be known through His revelation or not at all. Hence metaphysical knowledge depends upon whether one is willing to trust; revelation depends upon whether one responds in faith or in unfaith.

One cannot be compelled by the introduction of new evidence or by logical reasoning to change one's basic faith, in either of the above senses. John Hick has pointed out that "there may well, of course, be psychological limits to the persistence of challenged and discouraged faith, limits which will differ in each individual. But is there any *logical* terminus, any definite quantum of unfavorable evidence in face of which it would be demonstrably irrational to maintain theistic belief? It does not appear that there is or could be any such agreed limit." [9] Likewise, on the other hand, a philosopher who defends the verification principle could never be compelled to accept the proposition that God exists by any quantum of factual or logical evidence.

These observations may not help one to decide which metaphysical views are true, but they do help one to see why it is

that philosophers disagree without having to resort to explanations which impugn their competence, without attributing their
disagreements either to simple factual or logical blunders or to
clashings of the unconscious, and without falsely explaining away
their real disagreements.

It has been argued that explanations in terms of factual and/or
logical mistakes or in terms of views which deny that disputes
are real are inadequate because it is implausible that philosophers
of demonstrated competence would have made the errors alleged
and would have persisted in them in the face of philosophical
criticism. The fact that *what is seen as an error by one philosopher is not admitted to be an error by another* indicates that
what one takes to be truth is a function of one's basic philosophical convictions, a fact which has very important consequences
for understanding metaphysical method.

An attempt has been made to account for the persistent disagreement of metaphysicians in terms of the complexity of reality,
the varieties of levels of experience and of plausible keys to the
nature of reality, the influence of various sorts of philosophical
conditioning, including grammatical structures, truth criteria and
ways of perceiving, and the general rootedness of metaphysical
theories in "faiths."

In the chapters which follow, attempts to bypass basic metaphysical questions will be discussed, preliminary to an exposition
of metaphysical thinking. Discussion both of naturalism and of
appeals to religious authority is undertaken in order to show
that neither approach is able to escape the basic metaphysical
inquiries.

II. Basic Disputes Are Factual

The claim that basic metaphysical disputes should not be regarded as mere matters of logic was advanced rather incidentally in the preceding chapter. The claim was supported in two ways, by the prima facie implausibility of the supposition that otherwise competent philosophers make *and persist in* basic logical errors, and by the plausibility of the observation that philosophical disputes are often disputes as to whether some method or logic is the final criterion in philosophical discussion. Logics or methods are matters in dispute in philosophy, not criteria for settling disputes.

Such a claim requires further treatment, particularly since there are philosophers and theologians who would not concede it. Many classical philosophers have held that there is only one logic and only one sound philosophical method. Classical philosophers are not alone in this claim either, for there is a decided tendency among philosophers whose inclinations are toward naturalism to assume the same finality for a different method, and many theologians have yet different authorities. Thus there is need for further treatment of the question as to whether basic philosophical disputes are logical or factual.

The answer to this question might seem at first glance to be obvious since philosophical theories are theories about the real facts and are thus to be evaluated in terms of their adequacy as descriptions of those facts. However, there are those who would hold also that logic or method itself provides a criterion for truth and untruth. That is, a classical rationalist would hold that the conclusion to a logical argument is *ipso facto* true, as well as being a valid conclusion from two premises which together logically imply it. Moreover, naturalists, at least those whose positions are dealt with in the discussion to follow, seem to say at least sometimes that a nonempirical proposition is not merely unprovable (perhaps a legitimate claim) but *ipso facto* false. Thus, in both cases, appeal to a method is used to decide questions of truth because conformity to a particular method is being used as a criterion not of validity but of truth.

If, however, this is fundamentally a wrongheaded procedure, if instead of deciding questions of truth about facts in terms of appeal to a method one decides questions of the adequacy of methods in terms of appeals to facts, basic questions turn out to be primarily factual rather than logical. In the discussion which follows, this issue and related ones will be explored.

The first task is to show that the adoption of a naturalistic method as a final court of appeal in matters metaphysical is at the same time the adoption of a naturalistic metaphysics and the exclusion of some (perhaps all) nonnaturalisms by means of this methodological decision. In short, to be naturalistic in method is to close oneself to certain metaphysical views the truth of which is logically possible on any candid view. Notice should be taken that in the discussion here reference is made merely to what is possibly true about the real facts; there is no claim that such things really are true. There are obviously more things in our philosophy than there are in heaven or earth, and here the discussion concerns merely what is possible.

The Bias of Naturalistic Method

The claim that naturalistic method is philosophically neutral has been made by Sidney Hook, who argues that "scientific

59290

LIBRARY
College of St. Francis
JOLIET, ILL.

method does not entail any metaphysical theory of existence, and certainly not metaphysical materialism"; he goes on to add that scientific method is "the only reliable way of reaching truths about the world of nature, society, and man." [1] Now the basic question is: Is this claim true? Is the statement that scientific method does not entail any metaphysical theory of existence a true claim? This depends upon what is meant by "scientific method." If one means merely by this claim that all truth claims ought to be tested in some appropriate way without specifying any criterion for appropriateness, one might rule out little or nothing by adopting it. However, if one means, as Hook clearly does and as is customary when speaking of scientific method, some sort of appeal to sense experience and to what is publicly observable, then a large number of possible truths about unsensed or unsensible entities are ruled out by his statement and the adoption of that method as a criterion for reliable truth entails the exclusion of some views and the inclusion of only those theories which claim that there is nothing which is in principle unverifiable in terms of scientific method.

When Hook goes on to claim that "for every traditional conception of God, the weight of evidence so far is decidedly in the negative," or that "no plausible evidence has been found to warrant belief in the entities and powers to which supernatural status has been attributed," therefore there is no justification in believing in them,[2] he shows that in fact he *has* rejected the kinds of bases upon which theology and metaphysics have traditionally been built. This suggests that "scientific method" as Hook uses it *does* entail a particular range of metaphysical theories of existence, that his definition of scientific method has implied a particular class of metaphysical systems which exclude both classical metaphysical systems and classical theologies.

The same kind of restriction is even more obvious in Sterling Lamprecht's discussion of naturalism and religion, both in his claims that to suppose there are bifurcations in nature, such as that of mind and matter, "is to become at once mythological," and in his affirmation that naturalism "would explain mind and purposiveness or any other thing or event or quality in the same way in which it would explain cyclones or wars or northern lights." [3] Obviously there exist metaphysical views which would deny the legitimacy of this methodological decision; hence it is clear that this decision *does* imply a particular range of metaphysical theories and does exclude others.

The methodological bias is further brought out when Lamprecht claims that appeals to revelation are not valid because such an appeal "of course begs the point at issue from the outset." He also claims that the traditional arguments for the existence of God not only fail but cannot be rescued through combination with empirical methods because it is "questionable whether the world-as-a-whole can ever be the subject of empirically justifiable propositions," and "applied to the world-as-a-whole the word 'contingency' (like any other word) is of dubious significance or perhaps of no significance." [4] Hence the usual theological claims are ruled out methodologically, by a decision about meanings of words which cannot be justified on purely logical grounds.

To these statements it must be said that to *exclude* the possibility of revelation "of course begs the point at issue from the outset," for to assume that there is no such thing as revelation is to exclude the possibility that certain forms of theism are true. The existence of God seems possible logically, and it is logically possible that this God reveals Himself personally to man; hence a negative answer cannot be given on logical grounds. Similarly, the meaning criterion Lamprecht adopts is such as to rule out legitimate logical possibilities, a point that will be returned to again.

The foregoing writers do not even seem to see that their

criterion is problematic. Ernest Nagel, however, does, and tries to defend the thesis that naturalistic method is unbiased, but without success. Remarking on the charges made by critics that naturalistic method is biased against the possibility of super-natural beings, Nagel claims that "the logico-empirical method of evaluating cognitive claims to which naturalists subscribe does not eliminate by fiat any hypothesis about existence for which evidence can be procured, that is, evidence that in the last resort can be obtained through sensory or introspective observation." [5] He goes on to point out that hypotheses about transempirical causes are perfectly legitimate so long as they imply statements about empirical data.

However, Nagel is not being completely candid, as the following two considerations show. In the first place, he says that naturalists cannot acknowledge claims to revelation, "not because their commitment to a logical method prevents them from treating it seriously, but because independent inquiry fails to confirm it." Obviously their commitment to a logical method prevents them from accepting anything which is not confirmed by *independent* inquiry, thus precluding any appeal to self-authenticating revelation. Moreover, he stipulates that "claims to knowledge must be capable of being tested; and the testing must be conducted by eventual reference to such evidence as counts in the responsible conduct of everyday affairs as well as of systematic inquiry in the sciences." [6] Now this statement seems to be neutral, but reflection shows that it is not, for Nagel neglects to point out that there are hidden principles which drastically restrict what is allowable in terms of naturalistic method. Although he says that hypotheses about transempirical causes are perfectly legitimate, he must be aware that their legitimacy would be denied on methodological grounds, in particular by means of an appeal to the principle of parsimony as in the following case.

Herbert Feigl, in a dialogue on the use of religious experience as evidence for the existence of God, puts the following point in the mouth of his empiricist. Suppose any situation in which a phenomenon is attributed to supernatural causes, but which can also be fitted into the categories of naturalistic explanation, "anyone adhering to the principles of scientific method would thereupon abandon the first hypothesis as superfluous. Just remember the principle of parsimony already formulated in Occam's razor: *Entia non sunt multiplicanda praeter necessitatem* or in Newton's first *regula philosophandi*." [7]

Suppose one admitted, as some theologians would, that acts of God seem to the unbelieving eye to be mere natural events, hence that the unbeliever *would*, however wrongly, explain acts of God by means of ordinary naturalistic categories, then, in such a case, the adoption of Occam's razor would lead to falsity. Thus, to assume that Occam's razor yields the whole truth is to assume that there is no God. [8]

Feigl is thus being honest when he has his theologian observe that the rule of parsimony is a rule of scientific method and that its use as a criterion is therefore dogmatic. [9] He concludes his dialogue in such a way as to leave the impression that the dispute never ends because there are no logical grounds for resolving it, a conclusion which seems to be correct.

Nagel's claim about openness is therefore false since if the requirement of appeal to "such evidence as counts in the responsible conduct of everyday affairs" does not get the transempirical cause then parsimony will. These twin weapons exclude methodologically a number of metaphysical entities the existence of which is logically possible, and Nagel is guilty of predeciding factual questions by adopting scientific methods.

Such remarks as the foregoing do not, of course, undermine naturalism as a metaphysical position. Comment has been made merely on its claim, by no means essential to naturalistic metaphysics, that its method is the sort of neutral criterion that ought to be accepted by all reasonable men as the only reliable method in philosophy. The point is that appeals to methods cannot justifiably be used to settle questions of fact; rather, appeals to facts must be used to settle questions of method.

Neo-Thomism vs. Naturalism

In addition to the reasons adduced in this present section, there are other reasons why the existence of the God of ordinary theism cannot be established by means of an appeal to naturalistic method. In Chapter Three the claim that there are empirical cases which could serve to verify or falsify theism is rejected. In the foregoing section the use of Occam's razor, the principle of parsimony, and the ruling out of bifurcations in nature and of revelation constituted a methodological refusal of conclusive tests for theistic assertions. At present, however, concern is with the type of claim made about God and knowledge of Him by classical and neoclassical philosophers and theologians, in order that the thesis of this chapter that basic disputes are not logical but factual may be illustrated.

There is a school of contemporary philosophers, known frequently as Neo-Thomists, who maintain the traditional claim that the existence of God can be proved. E. L. Mascall, for example, claims not merely that the human mind is capable of grasping things "in their ontological nature and so apprehending them in their dependence upon an infinite Being, which, as St. Thomas says, all men call God," but also that "it is a fairly safe generalization that all human beings unless they are blinded by prejudice or sophistication, *have* a conviction . . . of the existence of something which as a matter of fact is God." [10] Knowledge of God is not derived, allegedly, through inference, hypothesis, or conjecture; rather God's existence is "apprehended in a cognitive act." The mind apprehends "finite being as what it really is, as existent and yet not self-existent, as effect-implying-cause." [11]

Austin Farrer, likewise rooting knowledge of God in an awareness, states that "our cause depends on some awareness of substantial being, other than a mere awareness of phenomena and of their phenomenal order." "Finite objects of experience . . . *force* the mind to take them as shadows of absolute being, or *drag* the mind through the motions of thinking the absolute in thinking of them." [12] Again stress is put upon an awareness, but an awareness which is not merely "empirical" awareness.

However, knowledge of God is not based on pure logic either. F. C. Copleston points out that the classical arguments for the existence of God do not depend on logical analysis but rather on metaphysical analysis. He claims that Aquinas did not mean to regard the proposition "there are things which come into being and pass away" as *logically* entailing the proposition "there is an absolutely necessary or independent being," but he rather meant that metaphysical analysis of what it objectively means to be a thing which comes into being and passes away shows that such a thing must depend existentially on an absolutely necessary being.[13] Hence the cosmological argument is presented as neither an empirical one nor a logical one but a metaphysical one. It is ultimately a factual, not a logical, claim that God exists.

This means that such philosophers are rejecting the claim that there are only two types of proof, empirical hypotheses derived from sense data, and logically necessary propositions which are purely formal. They claim that there are necessary propositions which are nonformal, the necessity of which are shown by metaphysical, not empirical or logical, analysis. To point out, therefore, that such propositions are neither empirical nor logical is to point out something that the Neo-Thomist already knows and in fact insists upon.

It is not legitimate, therefore, to claim that because theistic arguments are neither empirical nor purely logical these arguments are logically invalid. Sidney Hook, in an attempt to show that the notion of God is "incomprehensible," that theism is full of "insuperable, intellectual difficulties," and that the "idea of a transcendent God has certain root *logical and linguistic* difficulties" which make it untenable, is able to produce only the following kinds of arguments, none of which are strictly logical arguments however legitimate they might be as other kinds of arguments.

What does it mean to say that something necessarily exists? It means that our knowledge of its existence cannot be the conclusion of an empirical or inductive argument, for such can only lead to a probability judgment. Nor can our knowledge be the conclusion of a formal deductive argument—unless the premises are taken as absolutely or necessarily true, which is never the case even with propositions in geometry.[14]

Hook's argument here causes not the slightest logical difficulty, at least if the Neo-Thomist position has been fairly expounded above, because the Neo-Thomist does not claim either kind of certainty for his propositions about God's existence. That is, his case is built neither upon conclusions of empirical or inductive argument nor upon formal deductive arguments. His argument rests upon a metaphysical analysis of what it means to be a thing which comes into being and passes away; such arguments are logically possible, just as the existence of God is logically possible.

However, Hook could reconstitute the argument on some other basis, but this would mean conceding that the debate is an extra-logical one, the contention with which the analysis undertaken in this chapter began. Such a reconstitution might proceed in the following way, beginning with a recognition that the points at issue, namely the question of the existence of God, of the nature of finite things, and of what kinds of proof are needed to establish basic metaphysical propositions, are all *factual* issues.[15]

Properly stated, then, the issue between Hook and Neo-Thomism is one as to whether reality is such that metaphysical analysis leads to the conclusion that God exists. If it does not, then the third type of proof used by Neo-Thomists might be an empty possibility, one that has no usefulness in metaphysics. Thus, Hook might say, given other worlds, real facts other than those of the world we inhabit, other types of proof might have been useful, but in our world they are not. This argument, however, is clearly not an argument in logic.

Bertrand Russell, with his usual candor, states this issue correctly when he remarks, "I do not pretend to be able to prove that there is no God." [16] He of course goes on to say that he finds no reason to believe that there actually is a God, but his remark indicates that he holds that this question is a matter not of logic but of something else. Russell is thus rejecting claims that this question can be decided by appeal to logic, a wiser position than that taken by these other naturalists.

Hook's other "insuperable" difficulties fare no better. He objects to any causal arguments for the existence of God on the "logical" ground that when theists argue for creation *ex nihilo* their use of "cause" is illegitimate because "in our experience nothing is or can be created out of nothing." [17] However, here again is posed an issue which is not a logical one.

No logical criterion enables one to answer the question as to whether things are created *ex nihilo*, and thus no logical criterion enables one to decide whether the words "cause" and "create" can legitimately be used in the theistic way. The question is a factual one, and is to be answered in terms of how things are actually created.

Perhaps creation *ex nihilo* is actually an empirically meaningful notion even though experiencing one's own creation is not possible. One might travel in space to the center of the universe at which, some astronomers suggest, such creation is taking place, or one might travel to the outer edge of our universe and watch God creating things there. On either example, Hook's objection that in our experience all cases of creation are those involving preexisting material is seen to be merely a statement about the physical limitations surrounding present human experience, limitations which could be transcended. Hence the difficulty he is raising is not a *logical* one.[18]

The logical problem, in a more generalized form, is stated by Dorothy Emmett when she observes that, although there may be some unitary character or relation which can be formulated univocally, nevertheless "if the metaphysical nature of the world should be that of the relation of finite existent to an *absolute* existent, the absolute existent would be *sui generis* and *in principle* could only be described analogically." [19]

The question as to whether there is a necessary being (metaphysically necessary, not logically necessary) is likewise a factual question. John Hick claims that "both the Biblical exemplars of religious belief and the great theologians of the Western world have employed a notion of God as factually (rather than as logically) necessary." [20] He goes on to argue that both Kant and Anselm used this notion and that it is clearly supposed in Aquinas' third way. A factually necessary being, then, is logically possible and there is no logical objection to the phrase "necessary being," if it is used in this way.

The problem referred to in the foregoing pages is sometimes stated in a different way, a way which makes the same point but in more familiar language. Sometimes it is pointed out that different metaphysical systems rest upon different postulates or presuppositions as to what the facts are. Regis Jolivet uses this

language in claiming that the Kantian critique of classical arguments for God's existence gets into the following difficulty:

It should be noticed that if it is affirmed *a priori* that cause and
effect can only be expressed univocally, this at once plainly begs
the question—the very offense of which the proofs for God are
accused. It is precisely the question whether they are univocal which
we have to discuss, and to decide this from the beginning is to
abandon the problem.

Again, when Kant asserts that all causal series which appear to us
in phenomena are derived from the *a priori* forms of sensibility and
understanding . . . in fact he only repeats without proving it, the
empiricist postulate of his whole system.[21]

Jolivet then goes on to argue something which seems to be true,
that the great majority of philosophers have in fact opposed this
empiricist postulate and have supposed that human thought can
penetrate beyond phenomena to the very being of things.
Whether or not one thinks that what the majority of philosophers
have thought is decisive, the point is well taken. Empiricism
does rest upon empiricist postulates, as Neo-Thomism rests upon
its own postulates. The crucial issue is the one of facts: What
sort of world is there? Which set of postulates enables an
exhaustive description of the facts?

There are several reasons why it is only to be expected that
basic questions are factual. Firstly, it is quite unlikely that philosophers and theologians are so foolish as to make simple logical
errors and persist in these errors even after they have been
identified. Secondly, since metaphysics is primarily concerned
with descriptions of the facts and only secondarily concerned
with logic, it is to be expected that the basic issues will be factual
and not logical ones. If the *facts* could be agreed upon there
would be no basic quarrels among metaphysicians. Thirdly, the
question of the *existence* of anything, animal, vegetable, or min-

eral, is a question of fact not of logic. The existence of God is logically possible; whether God exists or not is a matter of fact and ought to be discussed on the level of fact.

Summary and an Additional Comment

The purpose of the foregoing observations has been to illustrate the claim that methodological assumptions often mask metaphysical faiths. Employment of rules should be accompanied by an implicit or explicit hypothetical proposition; *if* the facts are such that this rule is an adequate criterion for metaphysical truth, *then* certain conclusions can be accepted as true. Metaphysical disagreement can be seen as the debate as to which set of fundamental premises is true, and all observations must be made with the disclaimer stated above.

The oft-made claim that there is a radical difference between empirical and *a priori* methodologies must be seriously qualified because of the reasons given above. Of any empirical system it must be said that observation can give the whole truth if and only if the premise that there are no unobservable entities is true; hence conclusions reached about the nonexistence of unobservables are in this sense already contained in the premises, and if the premises are mistaken the conclusions are not proved.

Of course one might pull in his horns and claim less, perhaps making the uncontroversial claim that science merely yields knowledge which can be known by means of a particular method, without going on to say anything about the possibility that there are other methods which give additional truth. Such a statement would be perfectly valid and metaphysically neutral. However, the statements of the naturalists cited above surely go beyond this restricted affirmation, and it is in so far as they go beyond this that naturalism has been treated as a metaphysic.

The point is that naturalism is not neutral metaphysically, but this does not imply that naturalism is an inadequate metaphysical view, for a good case can and ought to be made for naturalistic metaphysics. The point is merely that it *is* a metaphysic and that it must be argued for in the way in which any metaphysic is presented and defended.

Surely the success of naturalistic method in the sciences constitutes a powerful argument for naturalism. Moreover, naturalism is able to provide, in a way which other systems cannot *ex hypothesi*, "showable" results. Theists cannot point to God, nor idealists to cosmic mind, and classical philosophies have been unable to provide proofs which are convincing to many modern minds. A scientist, however, *can* prove his *positive* results to everyone's satisfaction, at least in principle. For example, he is able to show that religious experience is related to psychological and sociological factors. The theologian may claim, quite rightly, that the naturalist cannot prove that there are no additional factors—but at least the naturalist *can* prove that there *are* naturalistic factors and the theologian cannot make his case so clearly. In brief, the naturalist can prove his positive points to everyone's satisfaction and no one else can do so in the same concrete way.

In the chapter which follows, two important claims about theological language will be examined, the claim that theology is not metaphysical and hence is not subject to metaphysical criticism, and the claim that religious beliefs ought to be subject to empirical verification or falsification. The conclusion reached is that both claims are false, that theological claims are metaphysical but nonverifiable at least as that term is usually meant. The stage is then set for discussions of metaphysical method and of metaphysical and religious symbols.

III. Theology Is Metaphysical

It has been argued that basic metaphysical disputes cannot be resolved either in terms of appeals to a neutral logic or in terms of appeals to "plain facts," for basic disagreements are often disputes over logic, for one thing, and the kinds of facts to which disputants appeal are not any commonly agreed upon set of "plain facts" but are rather interpreted facts, for another.

In the present chapter an attempt will be made to illustrate these claims by means of an investigation of two problems much under discussion in both theological and philosophical circles, namely, whether or not the existence of God is "verifiable" and whether or not a negative answer means that theism is not a genuine metaphysical position. A look will be taken at the further contention of some theologians that their claims are not really philosophical claims at all. The discussion centers on Christian theism because that is the context of the contemporary controversy being surveyed.

In the course of the chapter three important claims are made: (1) that the kind of theism under discussion cannot be validated by means of the "verification principle"; (2) that theistic claims are nevertheless factual claims; and (3) that theism claims factuality for its views, hence is one metaphysical view alongside others. It responds, as do other views, to internal and external criticism, changing in some degree with the times by incorporating new ways of thinking about old problems. No theism in its present form emerged full-blown from anyone's brow. This is

true of philosophies based on a fundamentalist interpretation
of Christian scriptures as well as others.

Theism and the Verification Principle

There has been much discussion in recent years as to whether
Christian theism can meet the terms of the "verification principle," that is, roughly, whether theism can be verified or falsified in terms of appeals to sense experience, and, secondly,
whether its inability to be so would constitute a disqualification
of theism as a serious philosophical possibility.

It is not important here to try to arbitrate among competing
views as to how the verification principle ought to be stated,
nor to enter into an examination of its general defense and/or
critique, neither being necessary for the discussion at hand. It
is important to show that Christian theism cannot satisfy that
criterion however it is put, and that this means theists ought
to reject the claim that the verification principle is the final
criterion for truth claims.

The verification principle states that for a sentence to be taken
as meaningful one must have knowledge of those "conditions
under which the sentence will form a *true* proposition and of
those which will make it false." [1] It is understood that the conditions referred to must be items of scientific experience, connectible with sense data which are in principle available to all,
and it is understood that this criterion was to accomplish the
elimination of metaphysical statements of the kind usually made
by philosophers and theologians.

A number of attempts have been made to meet this criterion,
by attempting in a variety of ways to claim that theism can be
falsified or verified in terms of sense experience, and a few of

those ways are discussed below. In each case a reason is given
for concluding that the attempt is unsuccessful. This is not to
say that the issues raised are irrelevant to the truth or falsity
of theism, but merely that they do not lead to verification or
falsification in the required terms.

1. It is sometimes claimed that the existence of evil suffices
to falsify theism, but this claim will not stand examination for
at least two reasons. First, of any alleged instance of evil it can
be claimed that it is not really evil since God exists and guaran-
tees that the evil will turn to good in the long run. What is
needed to falsify the usual theistic claim that there is an all-
good and all-powerful God is an instance of absolute and utterly
useless evil, but it is not clear that there is one. One would have
to disprove the existence of God in order to prove that any
instance of evil is absolute; hence this appeal is clearly circular,
presupposing what it pretends to prove.

Secondly, the reality of absolute evil could be admitted by
some theists who would then merely go on to qualify their
doctrine of God's nature. There are theists who deny that God
is all-powerful, for example, and such theists could find absolute
evil and the existence of God quite compatible.

A discussion of evil would usually be entered into in any
evaluation of theistic claims, but the mere presence of "evil"
does not of itself falsify theism.

2. The attempt is sometimes made to use the alleged "viability"
or workableness of theism as decisive evidence for its truth.
William James, for example, offered such claims. However,
what "viability" could prove is merely that theism is viable,
not that theism is true. The unexpressed premise required to
make the argument work is that the viable is true, but how
could one hope to establish the truth of that premise without
invoking some cosmic rationality, hence some form of belief

in God? Therefore the argument is fallacious on the grounds that it begs the question.

While the viability of a religious hypothesis, as John Hutchison maintains, "may be taken rationally as one bit of evidence, among others, for or against any religious idea," [2] it cannot stand as a decisive test nor even be put in as central a place as the author of that statement puts it.

3. It is sometimes alleged that there are specific experiences which would constitute verification of theism, or, less strongly put, experiences the absence of which would falsify theism. Whether or not one wakes up again after death is sometimes cited in this connection. The troubles here are many, one being that there are theists who do not expect to wake up again, hence for whom absence of life after death would not constitute falsification, another being that the fact of waking up would prove only that one lives again after death and no more. Moreover, there are nontheists who expect to live again. A new birth, therefore, would not of itself settle the question of theism one way or the other.

Similarly, mystical experience and religious experience are compatible with both theism and nontheism; hence the occurrence or absence of such experience would not constitute verification or falsification. There are nontheists who accept the fact of mystical experience as an interesting and valuable psychological experience but hold that its occurrence perhaps shows merely something about the range of possible human experiences.

4. It is sometimes claimed that Christian theism makes certain claims about Divine acts in history, claims which could be verified or falsified by empirical means. Here again there are difficulties, for even if there were historical claims of Christianity which could be proved to be false, all that would be required to meet the difficulty would be a modification of certain his-

torical claims, and there are many theists who have already welcomed such modification.

However, the argument need not go this far because the historical claims offered by Christian theists are not the sort of claims which could be verified or falsified. Suppose that it could be shown by means of medical testimony and photographs that Jesus of Nazareth rose from the dead. This fact would not of itself verify theism, but merely a particular claim about history. A nontheist might very well be amazed that such things happen and begin to search for an explanation, perhaps in spiritualistic terms, but he need not accept theism as a result.

What is crucial for theism is not the presence of a historical event but the explanation of that event, not merely the resurrection of a body but the why and how of it. What is crucial is the evidence that the event is a *divine act*, and this cannot in principle be shown by means of an appeal to historical events.

Moreover, there are theists who do not tie their views so closely to specific historical events. It is not unusual to find even theologians, whose views would be basically the same independently of the results of any historical investigation, denying that there was a physical resurrection. Could the event be validated it would establish only the event, not its theological interpretation, and were it not validated it need cause only a modification of theism.

What is essential in each of the types of factual question mentioned above is not the "plain facts" but the question as to the proper interpretation of those facts. The occurrence of seeming evil is compatible with both theistic and nontheistic interpretations, as is the viability or lack of viability of religious views, the occurrence or nonoccurrence of afterlife and religious experience, and the truth or falsity of claims about historical events. Hence the facts in question cannot fairly be held to decide the question as to the truth or falsity of theism.

The matter can be stated in a different way. Were God the sort of being whose existence *could* be decided in terms of appeal to "plain facts," that is, were God observable through telescopes, He would not be the sort of God whom most theists are concerned to defend.[3] To propose verification in these terms is to propose a nontheistic answer however the test comes out. In fact, it would be the sighting of God in a telescope that would most dismay theists!

Is Theology Nonmetaphysical?

It is tempting at this point to suppose that theistic assertions are not factual at all, and sometimes this claim is made in the interest of defending the truth of theism. Several attempts to erect a wall of separation between theology and metaphysics will be discussed, after a preliminary statement of the fruitlessness of such attempts is noted.

Theology obviously makes assertions about the world, hence cannot be nonmetaphysical in the sense in which the term metaphysics is normally used. Moreover, as has been observed by Charles Hartshorne, "whether or not theological doctrines *ought* to develop in independence of metaphysics, they have not generally done so in the past."[4] Even Karl Barth has said that "as regards terminology, theologians have always lived by some philosophy, and in that respect they always will," adding that it is far better to canvass the question "as to what the theologians of the early period really meant to assert in the language of their philosophy" rather than to get into a Pharisaic froth because their philosophy was different from ours.[5] Thus theology and metaphysics have not been separated up to now.

1. Joseph Sittler, a contemporary theologian, has argued for the separation of theology and metaphysics by offering the following four statements:

The affirmations of faith are faith's affirmations about God.

They are, therefore, radically different from all rational metaphysics and cannot be derived from or immediately connected with metaphysical propositions.

The affirmations of faith are statements about God's revelation or self-disclosure; they do not pretend to speak from within God.

The affirmations of faith have a paradoxical character.[6]

It is important to the argument of this book to show that the distinction between faith's affirmations and metaphysical affirmations has not and cannot be maintained, that the affirmations of faith *are* immediately connectible with metaphysical propositions.

It should be noted that Sittler's second statement is cloudy in two respects. First, after stating that the affirmations of Christian faith are radically different from the affirmations of *rational* metaphysics, he passes in the same sentence to an exclusion of *all* metaphysical propositions whether rationalistic or not, providing no justification for this transition. Secondly, he combines two ideas which need to be separated. It is one thing to say that religious affirmations are not *derived* from metaphysics yet quite another thing to claim that they cannot be immediately *connected* with metaphysical assertions. The latter is not true, and Sittler's own subsequent words betray the fact that he himself affirms doctrines which are quite obviously metaphysical, although perhaps not rationalistic.

For example, Sittler defines faith as "an acknowledgement of and some degree of effective relationship to a super-individual reality." Faith, then, seemingly knows at least that a superindividual reality exists. He goes on to declare that all theological affirmations must be symbolic because they "belong to this world" and hence are necessarily of "a figurative and symbolic character,"[7] indicating that faith has a knowledge of God by which it is known that terms derived from the finite world are inadequate to describe Him. Moreover, he claims that "the affirmations of faith are statements about God's revelation or self-disclosure," apparently affirming a knowledge that God is a God who reveals or discloses Himself to man, a bit of metaphysical knowledge which is very important. In developing the notion that faith's affirmations are paradoxical, Sittler claims that God "is at one and the same time the Eternal and the One who is contemporaneously active in history," [8] which is presumably also to claim something metaphysical about the nature of God.

Every one of these statements not only *can* be immediately connected with metaphysical propositions but is itself a metaphysical proposition unless one employs a peculiar definition of terms. God is a superindividual reality; He is known to be beyond human powers of conceptualization; He reveals Himself to man in history; and He reveals Himself as active in history yet Eternal. To say that these are not metaphysical assertions is quite arbitrary.

There is yet another sense in which Sittler's claims are metaphysical. The fact that faith's affirmations can be used to reject rational metaphysics would seem to indicate some similarity in class between the two kinds of statements. To deny that it is raining one must know that something else is the case, and it is difficult to see how it could be otherwise with respect to metaphysical knowledge.

Sittler is not an isolated case, for the claims which he has made have been made many times, by Tertullian, Luther, Kierkegaard, the early Barth, and also, interestingly enough, by Pierre Bayle and David Hume among others,[9] all of whom claim that theology makes no metaphysical assertions. Obviously it would be impractical to attempt to prove here that each one of the theologians in the above list has actually presented metaphysical doctrines while denying doing so, but the case could be made.[10]

2. Richard Kroner has attacked metaphysics from another direction, assailing its appropriateness for theology. His attack here is directed specifically against the methods of a group of theologians who thought of themselves as empirical theologians, but it has wider scope and constitutes a rejection of metaphysical knowledge of God *in toto*.

The tone of his critique is indicated by his lament that "there are Quislings within the theological realm whose puppet governments yield ingloriously to the swollen power of experimental science." [11] At least the following things, according to Kroner, are objectionable in the methodology of these traitors:

Man arrogates to himself the right to command God as he commands energies and processes of nature, and to conceive of God as such an energy or process.

If one can discover how a thing functions, moreover, if one can arrange one's knowledge of its functioning in an exact way, then one becomes master of it. . . . He can compel the thing to function in such a mode that it serves his needs or desires.[12]

These criticisms are unjustifiable not only for the specific reason that Kroner is unfair to those whom he is attacking but also for the more general reason that it is a mistake to assume that because one knows how something functions, one is able to compel it to serve his desires. Two separate senses of "mastery" are being confused.

Another critic of empirical theology accuses these same theologians of failing to be empirical because they speak of man's relation to God in terms of man's surrender and passivity,[13] canceling Kroner's comment but indicating agreement with Kroner that scientific method and passivity are antithetical.

However, both claims about scientific method are mistaken, as a moment's reflection indicates. To understand something, to know how it functions, even to "arrange one's knowledge of its functioning in an exact way," *may* lead to mastery of that something, but it quite well may not. Understanding of the functioning of things often leads to an awareness of what *cannot* be controlled and manipulated, because one discovers things to which one must adjust or accommodate oneself.

Thus empirical method is not *ipso facto* inimical to theism. One might want to add that there is nothing particularly beneficial either, that the basic questions in metaphysics are ones to which empirical science does not provide the final answer, and this may be true. The point here is merely that no battles are lost by offering the claim that theism is metaphysical. There is nothing in metaphysical method which is antagonistic to theism, nor is there anything in theism which renders it nonmetaphysical.

3. Alasdair MacIntyre objects to the view that religious assertions are metaphysical hypotheses on the ground that the type of adherence which is given to them precludes their being hypotheses. He claims that to hold that religious beliefs are hypotheses is to falsify the way in which they are characteristically held. For example, "part of the content of Christian belief is that a decisive adherence has to be given to God. So that to hold Christian belief as a hypothesis would be to render it no longer Christian belief." He further points out that it is not proper to treat such beliefs as hypotheses since "we do not offer evidence for these statements, we offer authority for them." [14]

It must be noted that a very important question has been waived by MacIntyre, the question of whether or not the way in which a belief is held is a criterion of its truth status. It is not self-evident that language is *always* used properly, even though some philosophers and theologians seem to imply that it is. For example, MacIntyre claims that philosophy "has become the patient description and classification of all those ways of using language that are of logical importance," and that instead of rejecting theology as a whole philosophers are now concerned with the examination of religious "forms of speech," how believers use their words (172). Yet surely, no matter what the changes in philosophy, it is still necessary for *someone* to ask the question as to the *legitimate* uses of language, and this is a matter not simply of how believers *do* hold their beliefs, but rather a matter of how they *ought* to hold them.

Theistic claims are not hypotheses, MacIntyre asserts, because religious language finds its justification in terms of an appeal to some authority, not to evidence. "Every religion . . . is defined by reference to what it accepts as an authoritative criterion in religious matters" (199). For Christianity the authority is Jesus Christ. "We do not offer evidence for these statements [theological doctrines], we offer authority for them. We point to the state of the world as illustrative of doctrine, but never as evidence for it" (201). "We justify a particular religious belief by showing its place in the total religious conception; we justify a religious belief as a whole by referring to authority" (202).

Similarly Ian Crombie claims that theological doctrines are based upon "authorized parables."

The things we say about God are said on the authority of the words and acts of Christ, who spoke in human language, using parable; and so we too speak of God in parable—authoritative parable, authorized parable; knowing that the truth is not literally that which our parables represent . . . but trusting, because we trust the source of the parables, that in believing them and interpreting them in the light of each other, we shall not be misled, that we shall have such knowledge as we need to possess for the foundation of the religious life.[15]

In addition to the perennial problems associated with any appeal to authority, concerning such matters as how one knows which interpretations of the words and acts of the authority to accept, there are two particular problems involved in the appeal to this particular authority. In the first place, there are many who call themselves Christians who take issue with the plain meaning of many of the words of Christ. The language of Christ is the language of His time and was, so many theologians say, inevitably mistaken about many things. On the supposition that Christians accept the contents of their belief on the authority of Christ's words, one would expect to find all Christians believing everything Jesus said.

The second problem is that it is not clear that Christian theology *has ever been* based solely on an appeal to the authority of the words and acts of Christ. Leaving aside for a moment the appeal of early and medieval theologians to Plato and Aristotle and leaving aside the vigorous tradition of rational proof in Christian history, it is not even in the New Testament tradition to appeal to the language of Christ or to the acts of Christ as *authority* for believing in God. Jesus established no new religion, rather He is preached as the One who fulfilled God's revelation in history. It is because He fulfilled past revelation that He is proclaimed as redeemer. Appeal to revelation validates the claims made for Jesus, and not the reverse.

This point is not commonly recognized and requires more extensive treatment; however, it seems clear from a reading of the New Testament that Jesus is preached as the fulfiller of revelation or the One in whose life takes place all the things predicted by prophets of old. Thus the gospel writers use proof-texts wherever possible, the preachers in Acts do not cite Jesus' words but appeal to His actions as fulfillment of former prophecy, and Paul almost never quotes Jesus. The authority of Jesus, thus, is held by the New Testament writers on the basis of evidence, is based on *proofs* of His Messiahship or Divine Sonship. In

brief, one does not accept the apostolic testimony because of
Jesus' authority; one accepts Jesus' authority because of the evidence. MacIntyre, thus, has reversed the New Testament claim.

Moreover, in the period of the church fathers, in the great
systems of Origen, later of Augustine and of Aquinas, heavy
reliance was placed on the role of reason and evidence. Thus,
for MacIntyre to claim that "to ask for reasons for or a justification of religious belief is not to have understood what religious
belief is" (208) is to depart radically from biblical religion and
from all but the most recent Christian history. One wonders
who it is who has failed to understand what religious belief is.

Michael Foster has made a number of relevant observations
to this very point in addressing the status of "we" statements in
modern philosophy. He points out that such usage statements
are not philological statements nor are they based upon statistical
studies of the uses of language, and it seems to be true that "propriety in the use of language, in the sense of propriety which is
other than merely linguistic, is relative to the basic attitude which
the speaker assumes." [16] For a philosopher "the correct use, that
is the philosophically important use, for him is that which he can
adopt," [17] and statements such as "when we use the term x we
mean . . ." are advocacy statements, defending a certain use of
x as the philosophically significant one and rejecting other
usages. It is not the case that philosophical disputes are merely
disputes about usage which could be arbitrated by an appeal to
an acknowledged "correct" usage. Philosophical disputes often
are over what use of a term *is* the philosophically important one.
"We" statements are very much like "creedal affirmations," he
concludes. [18] Thus "we" statements are very much matters of
dispute, and it is not enough merely to indicate how "we" use
words.

But, this objection aside, it is not even clear that "to hold

Christian belief as a hypothesis would be to render it no longer Christian belief." It is quite clear that Christians *have* modified elements in their beliefs, that items of theology and sometimes even basic theological doctrines have been modified and even discarded when it has seemed no longer possible to hold them, indicating both that evidence is relevant to the retention of belief and that those beliefs which have been discarded, at least, were hypotheses which later thought has already rejected. It is customary in many religious circles to insist that beliefs are frequently revised in the light of scientific, philosophical, and religious criticism; [19] that Christians often refer to problems of radical disbelief and doubt also indicates the legitimacy of the use of the word "hypothesis" for religious beliefs.

One further corollary claim must be challenged and that is MacIntyre's assertion that there is no connection between religious language and other language, that not only can religion not be justified in nonreligious terms, it cannot even be *translated* into or elucidated in terms of nonreligious concepts. This view MacIntyre offers as what he calls the logical correlative of Barthianism in theology (203).

He claims, for example, that to "elucidate the notion of God we have already seen that any non-religious concept is inappropriate. And to elucidate it *via* the concept of God's existence is to attempt to elucidate it in just such a way" (203). His reasons for the exclusion of "existence" are two, that it is useless to assert God's existence because for those who believe it the assertion is superfluous, while for those who do not believe it the assertion is senseless; and that the word "exists" is inappropriate because its use implies that God is a superobject.

The first of these reasons is both beside the point and mistaken. It is beside the point because the question of the truth of a proposition is not decided in terms of whether or not one finds occasion to use it, and it is false because there *are* occasions in which this particular proposition is needed. The theist wants to assert not only that he believes in God but that God has reality external to the believer's mind, and the assertion that God "exists" is required to state this.

The second reason, the alleged inappropriateness of the assertion on the grounds that it contains the implication that God is a superobject, can also be countered. This assertion has been made throughout the history of religious philosophy without the alleged implication being drawn. Neither St. Anselm nor St. Thomas nor their philosophical opponents would have thought that God was being asserted as a "superobject," and there is no good reason to accept the claim now however stylish it may be in some circles.

As to his claim that there is no connection between religious language and other language, it seems that he is plainly mistaken. Religious language has always been continuous with other language not only in terms of the meaning of words but also in sentence structure. Barth's admission that "theologians have always lived by some philosophy," cited earlier, is an indication of this. Certainly both religious and nonreligious people have understood what sentences about God mean, and certainly theological sentences use structures and meanings borrowed from ordinary language.

Perhaps MacIntyre means to assert that the objects of theological thought and the objects of scientific thought are not the same. The case for this would be strong, at least according to some theological systems. But if this is his meaning, he states it badly in trying to assert absolute independence of languages. Similarly he states it badly when he tries to argue not only that Christian theology is based on authority but that all fields of thought are also so based. He claims that "of science and morals it can also be said that one can justify particular theories or prescriptions, but that one cannot justify science as a whole in non-scientific, or morals as a whole in non-moral, terms. Every field is defined by reference to certain ultimate criteria. That they are ultimate precludes going beyond them" (202).

This cannot be conceded because it implies that the ultimate criterion for any theory is the subject matter in which it occurs, not the objects to which it refers. It would be incorrect to say that moral theories cannot be justified except in terms of an appeal to how "we" use moral words. In science the proper appeal is not to what "we mean when we use the word *x*" but to the thing which *x* is used for. In short, we appeal to the things that language is *about*. We appeal to nature, not to definitions. Again, MacIntyre is making the illegitimate assumption that particular usages of language are *ipso facto* valid. To proceed this way is to proceed exactly backwards. The truth of language should be measured in terms of its descriptive adequacy, not vice versa. According to MacIntyre's criterion the facts of the world become something to be deduced from linguistic usages rather than correct usages being something to be discovered from the world. The final appeal in theology or any other field is to the facts and not to some religious usage or philosophical idiom.

Summary and a Concluding Comment

An attempt has been made to analyze two facets of contemporary discussion over Christian theism, the claim that theism can be verified or falsified in terms of the verification theory and the claim that theistic assertions are nonmetaphysical, hence exempt from metaphysical scrutiny. The conclusion reached is that theism is metaphysical but that its claims cannot be settled in terms of ordinary empirical cases. Moreover, it has been suggested that appeals to both the verification principle and the religious use of language are in need of metaphysical justification. Basic metaphysical disputes are disputes over truth criteria as well as disputes over facts, hence cannot be settled in terms which can be agreed upon by everyone.

Christian theism, then, is not unlike other metaphysical views. It appeals basically to certain facts or "interprefacts" as being fundamental for understanding the nature of things. Traditionally, appeal was made to miraculous events as convincing proof. Now, not simply for reasons of doubt as to the historicity of "miracles" but also because of increasing recognition that even if miracles occurred they would not be recognized as such by unbelievers, miracles are not used as proofs in the same way as before. In any case, the appeal to miracles, whether in the old sense or in the attenuated sense defended by many modern theologians, is an appeal to a certain perspective on fact. Evidence was furnished in the preceding chapter that the "proofs" for God's existence are now put forth in such a way as to show their dependence on factual experience. Modern appeals to revelation acknowledge the possibility that revelatory events and words can be interpreted variously according as one stands in faith or unfaith. Thus there is no escape from the claim that Christian theism is a metaphysical view beside other metaphysical views appealing to facts-as-seen-in-a-particular-perspective just as do other views, and subjecting its fundamental doctrines to the same internal and external scrutiny.

The time has now come for a full discussion of the nature of metaphysical thinking, for it has been shown that basic disputes in metaphysics are disputes over facts, though not "plain facts," as well as disputes over logic. Attention must be directed to the quest for a description of metaphysics which can account for the persistence of fundamental disputes without reflecting unduly on the competence of the disputants.

IV. The Nature of
Metaphysical Thinking

———◦•◦———

Up to the present it has merely been *claimed* that the clue to
the persistence of metaphysical disagreement can be found in
the rootedness of metaphysical theories in basic assumptions, in
what is often called faith. It has been argued that any more
simplified explanations of such disputes are inadequate, and
an attempt has been made to indicate what sort of analysis of
the relation between basic assumptions and rational systems
ought to be given. But the question of the nature of metaphysical thinking has not really been discussed in fullness and
it is to this task that our attention now turns.

The task of this chapter is to present and defend a particular meta-metaphysical theory, one which has a great deal of
support among modern thinkers of quite different persuasions,
to indicate both the method by which such theories are built
and the ways in which their truth is tested. Use will be made
first of a number of similar observations from diverse metaphysical traditions, followed by a full exposition of Whitehead's meta-metaphysical theory in an effort to present and
defend this theory as the most plausible one.

In the Introduction it was pointed out that a number of historical and philosophical studies have forced a searching reexamination of the status of metaphysical theories. Not only
have there recently been questions about the legitimacy of
metaphysics, stemming both from impatience over the lack of

final solutions to basic problems and from epistemological questions about the very possibility of metaphysics, but also specific
metaphysical theories have been subjected to searching criticisms. The old confidence in a universal system of truth,
whether based on pure reason and buttressed by revelation, or
based on scientific method buttressed by impartial public observation, is largely gone. Sharply challenged first by Hume
and Kant, later by the rise of relativity, especially as a result of
the emergence of a knowledge of history and its diversity,
scientific relativism in the physical and social sciences, and religious relativism occasioned by a searching criticism of traditional scriptures and theologies, plus an awareness of religious
pluralism, the view that there is a universal system of knowledge has been largely abandoned. It is the contention of this
chapter that a new consensus has been slowly emerging, a
new consensus not as to the *results* of metaphysical thinking
but as to the *method* of metaphysical thinking, a consensus
acknowledging intellectual relativity.

There are a number of reasons why thought is inevitably relativistic to a degree, the most important of which is that the
very tools of thinking, perception and conception, come to the
individual already formed metaphysically, already embodying
metaphysical predispositions.

With regard to conceptual language, W. M. Urban has
pointed out that language is already "metaphysized." A language has its pattern, implying a particular metaphysic, and
"a common inherited scheme of intuitions and conceptions lies
all around us and comes to us as naturally and unquestionably
as the air we breathe." [1] Alfred North Whitehead had a related
point in mind when he asserted, in discussing religion, that
"you cannot claim absolute finality for a dogma without claiming a commensurate finality for the sphere of thought within
which it arose." [2] To assert a single sentence as final is to claim,

implicitly, finality for a whole system of thought, since a single sentence embodies a linguistic and metaphysical structure and partakes in the adequacy and/or inadequacy of that structure.

With regard to perception, it must be pointed out that appeals to "fact" involve metaphysics, since "facts" are always facts-from-particular-perspectives. There is, it has been admitted, a common-sense meaning of "fact" which is relatively independent of metaphysics, but the kinds of facts which are important for world views are metaphysized facts. Susanne Langer has stated that *"a fact is an intellectually formulated event,* whether the formulation be performed by a process of sheer vision, verbal interpretation, or practical response."[3] It has even been suggested that the word "interprefact" is more proper than "fact."[4] Factuality is fact-for-some-particular-person, factuality-from-some-particular-point-of-view, and as someone has said, "this being the case, there is no such thing as givenness which is its own untouched and unqualified and ununderstood and uninterpreted self."[5] Views as to what the facts are vary widely, each metaphysic presenting its own version of the real facts.

Arthur O. Lovejoy once attempted to set down the types of cultural and psychological factors that affect views of reality. His claim was that at least the following types are important:

a) assumptions and mental habits; for example, the tendency to think in terms of simple categories rather than complex ones;

b) dialectical motives or very general intellectual habits such as types of logic; for example, nominalistic versus "flower-in-the-crannied-wall" logic;

c) susceptibility to various kinds of metaphysical "pathos"; for example, the pathos of sheer obscurity and the monistic pathos;

d) linguistic ambiguities contained in the sacred words of a period.[6]

Facts are already metaphysized, experience is already metaphysized, language is already metaphysized, and people are already metaphysized, hence the relativity of percepts and concepts to metaphysical predispositions.

It has already been argued that faiths cannot be separated from metaphysics, both in the sense that faiths must be stated in terms of language which contains metaphysical structures and in the sense that faiths imply metaphysical propositions directly. It must also be remembered that the reverse relation is also found. Particular metaphysical claims mask faiths. The adoption of a particular criterion of truth, for example, is at the same time the adoption of a particular kind of metaphysical theory, namely that kind which uses that sort of criterion. When one has decided on one's criterion one has already prejudged basic metaphysical issues. For instance, the verification principle as usually employed is the final arbiter of meaning if and only if the positivistic views which it reflects are metaphysically correct; hence its employment issues from a positivistic faith and, of course, tends to confirm its assumptions by yielding only positivistic conclusions.

Bias can even be built into basic definitions. Metaphysics as the quest for the nature of things can be defined in two ways, one of which involves considerable prejudgment as to what metaphysical possibilities are live. One may consider metaphysics as the quest for universal characteristics, a definition which contains the tremendous assumption that all realities have characteristics in common, or one may consider metaphysics in a more open-ended fashion as a concern with a description of the nature of all things, allowing the possibility that there are no strictly universal categories.

Similarly, it is wise to allow for the possibility that there may be several ways of knowing, and not merely one. Some philosophers have claimed that there are special sources of knowledge available only to the few, and this claim must be considered. These same remarks apply also to the possibility that there may be many levels of meaning for words. On some metaphysical analyses only literal meanings need be used, but on others, analogies and perhaps even equivocations become necessary. Although there *may* be some unitary character or relation which could be formulated only in univocal terms, as Dorothy Emmett has observed, nevertheless, "if the metaphysical nature of the world should be that of the relation of finite existents to an *absolute* existent, the absolute existent would be *sui generis* and *in principle* could only be described analogically." [7] Either to require univocity or to require analogy would be to predecide for some particular range of world views.

As the word "metaphysics" can be defined so as to mean either descriptions of total reality or descriptions of that which is universal to everything that is, so the words "naturalism" and "scientific method" can be defined in either an all-inclusive or a narrower sense. Scientific method is sometimes defined so as to be equivalent in scope with thinking itself, or it may be defined so narrowly as to mean laboratory science; there are also possibilities between these two. It is *possible* that laboratory science provides all of the knowledge which is relevant for metaphysics; however, to assume this at the outset would be to bias the inquiry.

A Modern View of the Nature of Metaphysical Thinking

There is a wide area of agreement concerning the nature of metaphysical thinking, as the following statements show. It is to be noted that although these statements have been made by exponents of widely variant metaphysical positions they indicate agreement as to the nature of metaphysical thinking itself. Paul Tillich, speaking of metaphysical systems, has pointed out:

One could say that in each system an experienced fragment of life and vision is drawn out constructively even to cover areas where life and vision are missing. And, conversely, one could say that in each fragment a system is implied which is not yet explicated. . . . A fragment is an implicit system; a system is an explicit fragment.[8]

A theory, thus, begins with some fragmentary insight and is constructed into a whole system, a system which is implicit in the initial fragment.

In similar words, John Herman Randall has stated:

On the basis of what experience and insight we may be granted, we frame some metaphysical hypothesis, treat it as a leading principle, and proceed to explore its consequences. . . . The value of a leading principle clearly depends upon whither we are led, and the only test of a metaphysical distinction or concept consists in the illumination and clarification it can bring to a wide variety of subject-matters—ideally, if we are seeking complete generality, to any subject-matter.[9]

Randall's claim, then, is that philosophical thinking begins with an insight, which is turned into a hypothesis, which is then used to illuminate every subject matter. The pattern is the same as in Tillich's descriptions—a fragmentary insight which is extended into a whole system, the test for the insight's usefulness being its capacity for extension and the degree of generality which can be achieved. Presumably insights that are not capable of complete generality are discarded or subsumed under insights that are capable of illuminating every subject matter.

Charles Hartshorne makes a similar point, approaching the matter in a slightly different way. His claim is that metaphysical descriptions are "set up as *questions* whose full meanings only deduction of the consequences of possible answers can tell us. . . . Thus self-evidence or axiomatic status is the goal of the inquiry, not its starting point." What is done in "metaphysizing" is the bringing out of "the meaning of tentative descriptions of the metaphysically ultimate in experience so that we shall be better able to judge if they do genuinely describe this ultimate." [10] The self-evident truth of metaphysical description, he notes, is discovered only at the end of the inquiry, not at the beginning. This suggests that there cannot be items of metaphysics which are accepted at once as unquestionable. Tentativeness should reign until completeness is achieved.

In an important and thoroughgoing book on metaphysics Dorothy Emmett argues that

metaphysics starts from the articulation of relationships, which are judged to be constitutive of an experience or experiences in a significant way. . . . A conceptual expression of such a relationship is then extended analogically as a co-ordinating idea, in terms of which further ranges of experience may be interpreted; or it is used in making a judgment concerning the nature of "reality." [11]

The description seems identical in content with that of the foregoing ones.

The most accurate name for this meta-metaphysical theory is provided by Stephen Pepper, who speaks of the "root-metaphor theory" of metaphysics. He claims that "a world hypothesis . . . is framed in the first instance on the basis of a rather small set of facts and then expanded in reference so as to cover all facts." [12] The original set of facts, the root metaphor, may of course undergo some transformation and refinement in the course of its expansion. Moreover, the metaphor may perhaps be discarded should it prove incapable of expansion, if, that is, it fails either of Pepper's proposed tests of "scope" and of "adequacy."

"Breadth" and "momentum" are the tests suggested by J. V. Langmead Casserley, who has suggested that in metaphysics "analogies are drawn from that realm of human interest and experience which the philosopher regards as most decisive and revealing," and then "the metaphysician takes up the task of empirical and experimental verification, transforming his analogies into hypotheses and testing them . . . for breadth and momentum." [13]

It is obvious that there are a number of different metaphysical theories which seem to their holders to pass the tests of breadth and momentum (Casserley) or scope and adequacy (Pepper) or self-evidence at the end of the inquiry (Hartshorne) or clarification of any subject matter (Randall). As a matter of fact, these thinkers differ among themselves as to which metaphysical theories pass the tests, but what is significant is that each of them provides the same sketch of the theory-making process itself.

A sketch, however, is not enough. The discussion requires a full picture of the process of theory building and testing. For this purpose the writings of Alfred North Whitehead will be used, because he provides a comprehensive treatment of the problem and also because his meta-metaphysical theory can be separated quite easily from his own world view.

Whitehead's Conception of Metaphysical Method

According to Whitehead, who provides a number of descriptive phrases, metaphysics is "the science which seeks to discover the general ideas which are indispensably relevant to the analysis of everything that happens"; it is the "dispassionate consideration of the nature of things," or "the endeavor to frame a coherent, logical, necessary system of general ideas in terms of which every element of our experience can be interpreted." [14]

This search for the basic ideas by means of which every element of experience can be interpreted proceeds in two ways.

There are two methods for the purification of ideas. One of them is dispassionate observation by means of the bodily senses. But observation is selection. Accordingly, it is difficult to transcend a scheme of abstraction whose success is sufficiently wide. The other method is by comparing the various schemes of abstraction which are well founded in our various types of experience (SMW, 19).

Amplifying this latter aspect of metaphysics, Whitehead has pointed out that "philosophy, in one of its functions, is the critic of cosmologies. It is its function to harmonise, refashion, and justify divergent intuitions as to the nature of things" (SMW, viii). With respect to the other aspect of metaphysical thinking Whitehead has noted that "when it comes to the primary metaphysical data, the world of which you are immediately conscious is the whole datum" (RM, 85). "I hold that the ultimate appeal is to naive experience" (SMW, 90), "to the general consciousness of what in practice we experience" (PR, 25).

However, the appeal to "naive experience" is troublesome since there is, according to Whitehead, no such thing as *uninterpreted* experience, and thus no possibility of a simple consultation of experience. "The first point to remember is that the observational order is invariably interpreted in terms of the concepts supplied by the conceptual order" (AI, 158-59). Presumably, although he does not in this context mention all these, Whitehead is referring to such things as the metaphysical orientation of the observer, the metaphysical concepts which are implicit in conceptual schemes and linguistic forms, and the validity which particular experiences are taken to have for different observers. In short, even "the relevance of evidence is dictated by theory" (AI, 222). On the other hand, it must be said that experience affects theory, for it is quite clear that observations modify the conceptual order as well.

As an illustration of the interaction between supposed simple "fact" and interpretation, Whitehead points out that the Papal Church, the Eastern Church, Wycliffe and Huss, Luther and

Calvin, Cranmer, Edwards and Wesley, Erasmus, Ignatius Loyola, the Socinians, George Fox, and the Vatican Council could with equal right appeal to history. "The conclusion to be drawn from the appeal entirely depends upon the value-judgments guiding your selection, and upon the metaphysical presuppositions dictating your notions of coherent theology" (AI, 168). This is an exaggeration since the claim that the conclusion "entirely depends" upon such judgments is extreme; however, the observation that different perspectives yield differing conclusions is unquestionably valid.

Rational criticism is necessary for the additional reason that our language is defective. Metaphysics is involved in a criticism of "deficiencies of language" which "stand in the way inexorably" (PR, 6). He writes also of philosophy as being imprisoned within language, a language which "is imperfect both in its words and in its forms" (AI, 229), so that "the very purpose of philosophy is to delve below the apparent clarity of common speech" (AI, 223).

Simple appeals to correspondence are thus ruled out for the twin reasons of inadequacy of language and, more importantly, because the facts one appeals to are already themselves metaphysized. He even describes philosophy as "the self-correction by consciousness of its own initial excess of subjectivity" (PR, 22).

In a discussion of religion his view of method becomes clear:

Religion starts from the generalization of final truths first perceived as exemplified in particular instances. These truths are amplified into a coherent system and applied to the interpretation of life. They stand or fall—like other truths—by their success in this interpretation (RM, 124).

Three emphases are here presented. The starting point is experience, the perception of truths in particular instances, the second is the amplification of these truths into a system, and the third is the extension of this system to wider areas of experience.

His other descriptions of metaphysical method say the same thing: "Speculative philosophy embodies the method of the 'working hypothesis'" (AI, 223). In metaphysics,

the true method of discovery is like the flight of an aeroplane. It starts from the ground of particular observation; it makes a flight in the thin air of imaginative generalization; and it again lands for renewed observation rendered acute by rational interpretation. . . . The success of the imaginative experiment is always to be tested by the applicability of its results beyond the restricted locus from which it originated (PR, 7-8).

The chief danger in such a method is that of overextension and overstatement. It must be kept in mind that metaphysical descriptions are tentative and hypothetical: "Metaphysical categories are not dogmatic statements of the obvious; they are tentative formulations of the ultimate generalities" (PR, 12). Finality can come only at the end, not at the beginning, of a metaphysical quest, if it comes at all.

But one does not proceed only in this way, by building up from creative intuitions; one also builds from established systems of abstractions. Metaphysics, since it is that area of thought concerned with "everything that happens," is concerned with harmonizing all the more particular sets of concepts such as the several sciences, art, religion, etc. Particular systems of abstractions describe particular aspects of the nature of things or particular kinds of facts; thus they are the result of particular selections from the wealth of detail presented in experience. Each more specialized discipline is an attempt "to formulate in precise terms the truths disclosed in" the particular selection from experience upon which it is based (RM, 58), and each of these schemes of abstraction furnishes evidence which must be taken into account in a metaphysical description. In one place Whitehead claims that philosophy "attains its chief importance by fusing [these particular systems] into one rational scheme of thought" (PR, 23). Whitehead did not believe that the fusion has ever yet been completed, for "we cannot produce that final adjustment of well-defined generalities which constitute a complete metaphysic. But we can produce a variety of partial systems of limited generality" (AI, 149).

Metaphysics must take into account all facts or alleged "facts" from all areas of human knowledge, and must attempt to work these into a world view which is adequate as a description of the nature of things. Whitehead would agree with Pepper's observation that a metaphysical theory "cannot excuse itself from taking any fact, comment, or criticism, into consideration on the ground that these lie outside its field, or its scope of inquiry, for the simple reason that by the definition of its enterprise, there is no outside of its field." [15]

That metaphysical descriptions are built upon abstractions, selections from the whole of experience, has its advantages since selection can be likened to cleanliness, "the removal of dirt, which is unwanted irrelevance" (AI, 265). Nevertheless, metaphysical theories *are* abstractions, based on selected instances and aspects of things; hence, in part, "the task of philosophy is to recover the totality obscured by the selection" (PR, 22). Put succinctly, Whitehead's position is that "every method is a happy simplification," yet "every simplification is an over-simplification" (AI, 222).[16]

Metaphysics as Confessional

Metaphysical systems, then, are attempts to describe the nature of things, and the final criterion for a metaphysical theory is its adequacy as a description. However, there are a great many difficulties in assessing adequacy, as the foregoing discussion has made clear.

One appeals to observation, but observation is modified by the conceptual order. One thinks, but thought is already metaphysically biased by the structure of the language with which one thinks. One tests claims to knowledge by appealing to well-founded systems of abstractions; however, the "well-founded" ideas may change in the process, and an additional danger is created by the fact that their very well-foundedness may occasion the overlooking of that which really fails to fit. Besides, which well-founded scheme should one take to be basic? Moreover, within specialized schemes of abstractions there may often be alternative models to choose between.

The upshot of it all is that finality occurs only at the end of the process of system building, for every element used to build with is tentative, subject to modification as the critical inquiry proceeds. However, even at the end a plurality of metaphysical systems is still found; hence the elements used achieve finality, if at all, only within that system and not universally.

It has been indicated that appeals to logic do not solve metaphysical problems because logics are a part of the fabric of systems which themselves require justification. Appeal to the plain facts is not sufficient since alternative theories as to the facts are presented by the various philosophies. Appeal to "self-evidence," to "authority," to "indubitability" is suspect since that which passes the indicated test varies according to whom one consults.

Theologians used to think that they had final answers provided by religious authority, but there is a strong tendency in modern theology to renounce that claim, as the following observations indicate. Two historians of Protestantism write:

Every religious institution, every creed, every pattern of worship, shares in the limitations and distortions (i.e., sin) of human exist-

ence. No religious pattern or form can be exempt from criticism
in the light of fresh apprehension of the truth. Though our apprehension of God in Jesus Christ may be an apprehension of
ultimate truth, it is still *our* apprehension and subject to the limitations of our perspectives as historically conditioned and as sinful
human beings.[17]

Two reasons for this criticism are indicated, not only the fact
that apprehensions of truth are historically conditioned, but also
the fact that these apprehensions are those of sinful man.

Characteristic of modern theology has been an increasing
tendency to reject the absoluteness of any doctrinal statement
of truth. Some measure of fallibility is attributed to Scriptures,
to Church, even to Jesus himself. All doctrines are held to be
subject to distortions imposed by perspective in space and time,
as the receivers of revelation shape their statements in terms derived from and sharing in the limitations of their age. Very in-
fluential in modern religious thought has been the conception
of the influence of man on religious truth suggested by Martin
Buber's statement that "the man, too, who is the 'mouth' of the
revelation, is indeed this, not a speaking-tube or any kind of in-
strument, but an organ, which sounds according to its own
laws; and to sound means to *modify*." [18] Not every one would
go so far as Daniel Day Williams has gone in the following
quotation, but many would. Williams claims:

Christian theology is an inquiry for the correct expression of those
truths which are discovered within the Christian movement and
which can be expressed in Christian symbols . . . but no presuppositions about the absolute or supernatural character of any portion
of the beliefs or objects of the movement need to be accepted as the
starting point. The theologian may legitimately inquire as to the
truth of any proposition which appears within the Christian fold,
and the nature and significance of Christianity itself may be a legitimate object of theological inquiry.[19]

Such a statement indicates the same lack of finality for theological statement that one finds for any other metaphysical formulation.

It is customary in these theological circles to speak of theological positions as confessional, that is, as positions for which truth is claimed but about which no strict proof is possible. Thus truth is "confessed," not established by strict logical or factual argument. In the light of the exposition of metaphysical method just completed, the appropriateness of this term for metaphysics seems evident.

There is no such thing as a neutral objective proof for metaphysical hypotheses, since the criterion for the truth of a metaphysical description, assuming its internal consistency and comprehensiveness, is its adequacy as a world description. Adequacy, however, is a function of perspective, of one's starting point, of one's basic judgment as to what is metaphysically significant in experience, of one's "faith." Metaphysical descriptions are "confessions" of the nature of things as seen from a particular perspective and are actually tested in terms of an appeal to the nature of things as seen from that perspective; hence there is a degree of circularity in metaphysical argumentation.

Metaphysical theories are changed infrequently, precisely because they must be comprehensive and adequate in order to be taken seriously as metaphysical theories. A world view, if it is genuinely a *world* view, provides an accounting for everything in the world, including the perspectives upon which opposing metaphysicians have based their theories. Because perception itself is conditioned by world view, and because evidence is evaluated in its significance as evidence in terms of world-view, it is very difficult to achieve a basic change in metaphysical theories.

The appeal of a metaphysical hypothesis depends upon the persuasiveness that the hypothesis has as an adequate description of the nature of things. A basic change in metaphysical description comes about when, for some reason, a description is communicated or discovered which is seen to provide a *more* adequate description than the one already held. Perhaps attention is directed to some relatively unnoticed aspect of things, or to some methodological or categorical assumption that has hitherto been accepted and which is rejected upon examination, or perhaps a whole new "gestalt" brings a meaningful solution to a host of problems and puzzles which had hitherto been troublesome. Such radical shifts can justly be spoken of as "conversions."

Thus it seems legitimate to state that the various metaphysical theories are each rooted in some basic judgment about reality, a fundamental faith in whichever of the competing metaphysical possibilities is to be trusted. Decisions cannot be said to be reached on purely rational grounds since varying faiths indicate varying criteria of rationality. Decisions cannot be said to be reached on purely factual grounds since varying faiths indicate varying views as to what is factual. Decisions cannot be said to be reached on grounds of metaphysical adequacy because what is seen to be adequate varies from system to system, from faith to faith, and is a reflection of what one puts one's faith in.

To suggest that philosophy is now played in a "new key" is to suggest that past certainties, be they those of "fact" or of "logic," have been dissolved—dissolved in the sense that there is now no consensus of the sort which has obtained in past ages, and dissolved in the sense that no one seems to have discovered any sure roads to a new consensus. There is agreement only that the philosophical key has changed. A new starting point involves philosophers, that of recognition of the crucial importance of basic assumptions. The crucial battles waged among philosophers have to do with basic assumptions as to facts and methods, not with the conclusions to be drawn from commonly accepted facts and methods. As Susanne Langer has cleverly stated, "Assumptions, generative ideas, are what we fight for. Our conclusions we are usually content to demonstrate by peaceable means." [20]

Not all philosophers have realized the situation. There are classicists who go on philosophizing as though Kant had never happened, and positivists who have not moved on to accept the later thinking of Wittgenstein, but they have no right to do so, as the various studies contained in this present writing show. Stuart Hampshire has observed that no philosopher now could follow Descartes, Spinoza, or Leibniz in looking for "general criteria" of truth or existence. He goes on to maintain that, as Kant and Wittgenstein suggested, we have to start "from the actual human situation which conditions all our thought and language, the situation, that is, of men observing and acting from a particular position in time and space, referring to particular things in their environment, identifying and classifying them, and trying to find ways to alter them." [21] Modern philosophizing recognizes no universals, no agreement as to facts, methods, or experiences. There are clearly many different views of facts, many proposed methods, many types of experience to be found.

Philosophical fragmentation is the rule; hence attention has turned to the reasons for philosophical pluralism, and one of the reasons which has become increasingly obvious is the confessional character of metaphysical theories. Metaphysical theories differ because they are based upon different fundamental assumptions as to how the world goes, each one confessing its own version of what is the case. These assumptions may be held critically or uncritically, and they may be changed through criticism and reflection, through the process of elaborating a consistent world view, or through harmonization of all the fragments of knowledge which seem well substantiated. However, at the end of the metaphysical quest the element of confession is still there. That it is still there is shown by the fact that competent philosophers disagree, after lifetimes of philosophical disputation.

It seems reasonable, therefore, to borrow some of the language fashionable among modern theologians, to speak of metaphysics as confessional, to speak of it as being made up of *kerygma* (proclamation) and *apologia* (persuasion), in recognition of the fact that the presentation of metaphysical positions involves both proclamation that this is the way the world goes and apologetic justification of the conclusions that it works this way. Such views are set forth for others to hear, to bring them to the faith. Likewise it also seems reasonable to speak of metaphysical conversion for those cases in which radical shifts of view occur, since taking on a new philosophical perspective or faith requires a drastic restructuring of a world view—percepts, concepts, and fundamental assumptions.

Of course it is possible to exaggerate this resemblance between theology and philosophy; however, the real danger is not that of overstatement but of understatement. Theology and philosophy have converged to a remarkable degree in recent times, and can no longer be set at opposite ends of a continuum as though they involved methods radically different in nature, as is done both when theologians sometimes decry philosophy as devil-sent and when philosophers decry theology as sheer subjectivity. Each thinker is theologian in that he confesses the adequacy of a particular faith, and philosopher in that he builds this faith into a rational system.

Metaphysical systems are elaborated and criticized extensions of faith. John Hutchison has proposed the following description of this relation of faith and rational system. He argues that, in any world view, two types of statement are evident.

The statements which are premises or assumptions and which function as foundations of the system are religious or mythical in nature. To them the mind gives that particular type of allegiance or trust which religion traditionally calls faith. Human reason then applies these assumptions or postulates to the most general structures and processes of the world, and philosophy, or more specifically ontology is the result. . . . Religion and philosophy seem thus to be related as Siamese twins.[22]

Such terminology as this serves to underscore the dependence of conclusions on starting points and provides a way of accounting for fundamental metaphysical disagreements which does not impugn either the logical ability or the perceptual abilities of philosophers. Philosophers disagree because they hold different faiths, because their views are formed by different languages and different assumptions, and perhaps because they commit themselves to different ultimates. No analysis which suggests that philosophical disputes are occasioned by simple factual or logical errors can do justice to man or his metaphysizing.

V. Symbols and Metaphysics

Symbolism and metaphysics are obviously closely related and the question as to what metaphysical symbols are basic is a primary philosophical question. Indeed, the adequacy of a metaphysical system must be evaluated partly in terms of the adequacy of the individual symbolic structures and rules which it generates, or which have generated it. The relationship works both ways since it is in part by the integrating and/or the extension of symbol systems that purification of philosophical ideas takes place; thus the critical process proceeds in both directions. Relatively adequate symbols are used to build metaphysical systems and the systems help to evaluate and improve upon the adequacy of the symbols.

It has become increasingly evident in recent centuries that the adequacy of symbol systems cannot merely be assumed, nor can it be tested in any sure way. David Hume, for example, suggested that many words used in ordinary philosophical discourse have no real counterparts in reality and proposed to do away with them. Kant, as is well known, tried to save some of these concepts, but by rooting them in the nature of mental process he raised profoundly the puzzle that has troubled philosophy ever since. How does one know that his mental processes and the tools by means of which man knows, his conceptual patterns and his perceptions, do not seriously distort the world? Since there is a human contribution to knowing, how can man trust his knowledge to be objective? If one attempts to appeal to the success of conceptual schema in ordering the world, then one is confronted by the difficulty that different people find different schema successful, and also by the fact that the schema themselves help shape the way the world looks.

Moreover, and here the difficulty is complicated still further, Kant indicated that conceptual schema useful in one field of thought might not be useful in another. Hence the answers arrived at by the scientific use of observation and reason may or may not be capable of extension into other realms. In brief, then, the success of a scientific model in terms of its adequacy to the qualities selected in science does not *guarantee* the usefulness of these same categories in the interpretation of ethics and theology. A set of concepts useful on a limited scale might be superseded when one moves into less limited realms. The failure of categories to be extendible might itself be evidence that these categories are not really adequate even for the realm in which they originated, or it might merely show that their usefulness is limited yet valid within these limits.

Moreover, to add yet another complicating factor, there may be areas of reality which are inaccessible to experience, in which the test of adequacy cannot be performed by any direct means. If God exists, for example, and is inaccessible to direct experience, then the adequacy of symbols of God's nature cannot be tested directly and some other criterion must be utilized to distinguish truth from falsity in this realm.

In this and the following chapter, an attempt is made to discuss metaphysical problems connected both with the structure of symbolizing and with the evaluation of particular symbols and symbol systems. Some basic characteristics of symbols are considered, special attention being given to the close connection between certain doctrines of symbol and particular world views, and to the special problems connected with certain kinds of religious symbols.

It is possible to say some general things about symbols without involving metaphysical decisions. On the meta-symbolic level one may discuss questions as to what a symbol is, what kinds of symbols there may be, what tests for the validity of symbols there might be, *how* symbols do their jobs, and so on, without making metaphysical decisions. However, if one goes on to decide what symbols actually are needed in a complete metaphysical description and what modes of reference these needed symbols have, then one has entered into metaphysical debate. Such questions as these latter ones cannot be decided short of the resolution of the basic metaphysical issues. Particular symbols, once linguistic contexts and interpretation rules are taken into account, imply metaphysical systems or parts of systems, and metaphysical descriptions are elaborate symbols or combinations of symbols. A completed metaphysical theory might usefully be regarded as a world symbol, and particular symbols and symbol structures might likewise be regarded as specific metaphysical hypotheses.

Symbol Systems Cannot Automatically Be Trusted

It has already been observed that part of the uncertainty attached to metaphysical views is due to the perceptual process itself, since perception is a compound of sensation and conception, thus is relative to both, and is perhaps distorted at both levels. To vary the language, one might say that uncertainty attaches to metaphysical descriptions because intellectual activity is symbolic activity, relative to mental and observational processes and perhaps distorted by both.

The following statements emphasize some of the difficulties in trusting symbols, besides those mentioned in previous chapters. Ernst Cassirer points out that because man uses symbols he can no longer "confront reality immediately." Man has so enveloped himself in symbolic forms "that he cannot see or know anything except by the interposition of this artificial medium." [1] One needs to add that symbol systems are also responsive to external reality, to the things which man is trying to symbolize with his words, a point which is made in Dorothy Emmett's description of symbolic activity. She begins with the claim that symbols describe something external to the self, going on to point out that "the mind is not a mirror, but a selective and interpretive activity which builds up symbolic constructions." Since the mind does interpret, there is a "possibility of originative response." Thus the relation of perceptual experience to nature is not to be thought of as that of "direct apprehension nor of likeness, but as a highly simplified and abstract projection which nevertheless bears some relation of systematic concomitant variation to the things projected." [2]

That there is some relation between symbol and the thing symbolized is shown by the fact that symbols change in an orderly way, that sense images of a tower, for example, vary in a systematic way according to changes in place on the part of the perceiver. That the relation may be a distorted one is indicated by the interpretive activity of the mind, by the fact that mind makes an "originative response." If distortion does take place, and if it takes place because the mind contributes an originative element, the resulting subjectivity might be extremely difficult to detect. It has already been noted that one of the chief tasks of philosophy is the removal of excessive subjectivity, but this task is complicated by the fact that even the language used to pursue metaphysics is itself "diseased," if disease there be. Friedrich Waismann points out that categories of interpretation such as "the notion of thinghood, of causality, of number, or . . . the way we render colour, etc." are already contained in our language. "Language, then, *contributes to the formation and participates in the constitution* of a fact; which, of course, does not mean that it produces the fact." [3] Thus language does not provide a completely independent check on fact because it helps to constitute what is taken to be fact. One is reminded of the biblical saying, "If then the light in you is darkness, how great is the darkness!"

It is easy both to exaggerate and to underestimate the difficulty here. The general semanticists seem to blame most of the ills of mankind on diseases of language, whereas there are those who trust language too much. One finds those who act as though they thought common sense to be verbally inspired, philosophers who defend classical Aristotelian philosophy in the same way, and theological conservatives who defend the infallibility of even the punctuation of the Scriptures, to give only three illustrations. It cannot be assumed that language is fully adequate, yet there must be some adequacy or else language could not be so fruitfully used.

Symbols and Meaning

A number of definitions of symbol can be found, but because narrower definitions beg crucial questions, the following is being used. Philip Wheelwright says that "a symbol, in the broadest sense of the word, is *that which means*; and the ways in which a symbol can mean are potentially as many as the ways in which one thing can stand for and lead the mind to something else." [4] This definition differs from two other widely used definitions, those which limit "symbol" either to mathematical symbols or to symbols which embody "an ideal content not otherwise expressible." [5] The latter definition is often used by theological writers who use the word "symbol" to refer only to those symbols which cannot be turned into concepts because they refer to things which transcend both physical and ordinary rational experience.

Although there may be some symbols which intrinsically resemble that which they symbolize, by onomatopoeia perhaps, there is a general consensus that symbols take on meaning by stipulation. Thus Humpty Dumpty is correct as to the origin of meanings. His remarks do not apply to developed systems of usages, since words take on standard meanings through shared use and through the creation of standard vocabularies, as in dictionaries.

Symbols mean in at least two ways, commonly called denotation or extension, the relation between a symbol and the objects to which it refers, and connotation or intension, which refers to the properties or qualities which are thought to be shared by those objects. A symbol thus denotes the members of a class of objects, the class which is connoted by the symbol. It is evident that, as connotation is made more precise, the number of objects denoted by a word is a function of the precision of its connotation. The denotation of "person," thus, would be confined to human beings if one connotation is specified, or could include angels and Gods on more inclusive connotations of that word.

Symbols stand for something both connotatively and denotatively, and, as has already been noted, they normally do so in an abstractive or selective way. A symbol does not ordinarily represent the whole of that which it stands for; it presents some significant selected aspect which can be used to stand for the whole. Thus symbols leave out something and that which the symbol presents should not be taken for the whole of that to which it refers. The usefulness of symbols relates partly to this abstractive function since irrelevant detail can often be omitted in talking about objects; however, one must beware lest the abstractions be reified and the fallacy of hypostatization be committed. Likewise one must remember that there are more things in heaven and earth than are dreamt of in our philosophy, since philosophy uses symbols and symbols are abstractions from larger totalities.

It does not seem necessary to include here a catalogue of fallacies in symbolism; however, two or three observations need to be made because of comments sometimes made disparaging the usefulness of symbols. It should be rather obvious that a knowledge of symbols does not substitute for a knowledge of the realities themselves, although the reverse statement, that a knowledge of reality does not always substitute for a knowledge of symbols, ought also to be emphasized. One is as likely to obscure the trees by looking at the forest as the reverse. Moreover, it would be fallacious to assert that because symbols themselves are static words they cannot refer to realities which are themselves dynamic, or to assert that because symbols are things they cannot refer to persons without "thingifying" them. The word itself is merely a vehicle for the presentation of an idea, and the characteristics of words need not be transferred to the ideas they convey. The word "whirlwind" is perhaps static; what it means either denotatively or connotatively is not static.

Of the various means by which the meaning of symbols can be learned a good deal needs to be said, for it is very easy to oversimplify. That meanings are sometimes learned by ostension, and sometimes by means of verbal definition, is generally admitted. However, some theorists go on to assert that some meanings are learned in other ways, for example, that some meanings are known intuitively. W. M. Urban claims that there is an *a priori* element in our understanding of the meaning of the name "God," and argues that "no empirical argument for God's existence can be formulated which does not presuppose an *a priori* knowledge of deity as an initial datum." [6] If God cannot be directly perceived, then the meaning of the words applied to Him must be derived by some such means, or else by analogy from things which can be directly perceived. Likewise it is a characteristic claim of Neo-Thomists that man has some "mental machinery" for thinking the notion of God.[7] Because, they claim, the meaning of such ideas as "necessary being" cannot be derived by analogy from finite experience nor defined by means of synonyms which are derived from finite experience, the idea must somehow be inherent in the mind.

Ostensive definitions themselves present problems since care must be taken not to limit the possibilities prematurely. G. E. Moore's views as to the "indefinability" of good and Rudolf Otto's similar claims for "the holy" are well known and need not be expounded here. Both claim that the meanings of those words can be gained only through having the requisite experience. W. T. Stace makes similar claims for mystical knowledge, arguing that the meaning of words used by mystics can be known only as one shares, partly or fully, in mystical experience.[8]

Thus, should one lack the required faculty or training or perspective to "see" what is being spoken of, there might be many symbols which are meaningful to some people and not to others who are excluded from understanding them because they lack the essential experience. The following observation, perhaps exaggerated, must therefore be taken into consideration:

Nothing, not even chairs and mountains, can be perceived until some social-historical development has brought forth the meanings in some community whereby our minds can distinguish and relate events in the way required to discern the chair or the mountain. Some primitive peoples would never perceive a chair, even though we put what we call a chair directly before their eyes.[9]

The ostensive definition of various shadings of tea tastes is dependent upon delicate sensitivity and practice, upon a higher degree both of perceptual awareness and of attention to elements within that awareness than the ordinary person has developed. Thus teatasters might use symbols the ostensive meaning of which cannot be known by the novice. Conceivably, then, there might be perceptions which are not available to the masses of men, and qualities which cannot be perceived by all men yet which can be pointed to by symbols for those who have such experiences. Thus when the Neo-Thomist claims to *see* that finite things are "effects-implying-cause" his case cannot be ruled out of court automatically. What one "sees" is a function of training, and even of metaphysical orientation, and different peoples seem to "see" things differently. Hence there can be symbols which are meaningful within one perspective but which seem meaningless to those who do not share that perspective. Thus one who speaks about a symbol as "meaningless" may merely be confessing his insensitivity to an experience shared by others.

Symbols and Contexts

No simple appeal can be made to ostensive definition to settle basic metaphysical questions about meaning since what is "seen" is a function of what one is trained to see and of what one's views allow one to see. This is another way of stating that facts are "interprefacts" or that disputes in metaphysics cannot be settled by appeal to the "plain facts."

There are additional kinds of context which must also be taken into account in learning the meaning of or checking the adequacy of symbols. Individual symbols cannot be abstracted from the structures in which they stand and from which part of their meaning is derived. Individual symbols are parts of

larger ones, for words are parts of speech and elements in propositions. Susanne Langer has observed that words do not stand by
themselves, they occur as parts of more complex terms such as
sentences and languages.

Grammatical structure, then, is a further source of significance. We
cannot call it a symbol, since it is not even a term; but it has a
symbolific mission. It ties together several symbols, each with at least
a fragmentary connotation of its own, to make one complex term,
whose meaning is a special constellation of all the connotations involved. What the special constellation is, depends upon the syntactical relations within the complex symbol, or *proposition*.[10]

Thus propositions are attempts to picture facts, and propositional
structures may vary from language to language, thus raising the
question of the adequacy of the syntactical patterns of whole
languages. However one-sided Whorf's position might be there
is certainly some truth in his assertion that "we cut nature up,
organize it into concepts, and ascribe significances as we do,
largely because we are parties to an agreement to organize it
this way—an agreement that holds throughout our speech community and is codified in the patterns of our language." [11]

The meaning of individual terms cannot be indicated in abstraction from their location in syntactical structures, and it can
be said that the explication of the meaning of an individual term
involves exhibiting the syntactical structure of that language,
which means showing forth its metaphysics at least in part. A
word has its meaning within a developed system of meanings,
and to assert that a particular language or system of meanings
can be used to describe reality is to argue that the metaphysics
enshrined in that system is sound.

Thus metaphysics, in one of its crucial aspects, is the search
for a language, a way of relating terms, that enables one to
think about the world without being deceived by the language

itself. The means by which the search is conducted—thinking and perceiving—are already formulated partly by prior perceptual and conceptual commitments enshrined in one's language and therefore are not metaphysically neutral. Thus one searches to eliminate distortion, using the instruments which have helped produce the distortion. Metaphysical thinking must question symbols and symbol-structures; it cannot merely assume their validity. An adequate language lies at the end of the metaphysical quest, not at its beginning, if it lies anywhere.

The rootedness of symbols and languages in fact must not be overlooked. Man does not merely converse with himself when he uses symbols, he converses about a world external to himself. By continued attention to that world he modifies his symbols and languages, and the usefulness of his language as a tool for mastering the world and for leading him to fruitful predictions about that which takes place outside him is an indication of a high degree of "fit" between his language and the world. It may be that language misleads, but it is surely more evident that language also leads.

Moreover, one of the most important clues to the adequacy of a metaphysical description must be its ability to lead one to a symbolism which seems to work. A metaphysics is tested in terms of the adequacy of the symbol system it generates, and this is probably the decisive test, since it is not mere formal consistency but adequacy that is the final criterion for metaphysical truth.

It is difficult to avoid overstating or underestimating the magnitude of the problem. The adequacy of a language cannot be assumed, and yet its usefulness as a language provides warrant for trusting in it. The function of terms in linguistic contexts affects the meaning of the term and the way in which the thing symbolized by the term is marked out, yet the meaning of the term is primarily controlled by the external object itself, and what the term exhibits primarily is not the syntactical structure in which it stands but the object or quality which it stands for. Thus connotation and denotation and the relation between them must be the primary concern in evaluating the adequacy of symbols, yet problems of context must also be introduced and really noticed.

Symbols and Interpretation Rules

Rules for interpreting symbols can be dealt with abstractly in a way which is independent of metaphysical commitment. One can treat rules as mere possibilities, for example, without prejudging crucial questions. However, if one begins to insist that certain modes of interpretation are logically invalid, then one has crossed over into a defense of particular metaphysical views. The point has been made already, in discussing whether basic metaphysical issues are factual or logical, that to insist that all metaphysical symbols be used literally is to exclude, methodologically, a number of important philosophical positions. Likewise, to rule for analogy, that is, to insist that reality is such that some metaphysical symbols *must* be used analogically, is also to exclude another set of positions. When one goes beyond listing and begins to advocate the necessity of certain rules then one enters the arena of particular metaphysical argument, as the following discussion indicates.

1. The *via negativa*, the "way of negation," so familiar to readers of mystical philosophy, is appropriate for metaphysical systems defending a qualitative otherness between God and world, or between reality and appearance. If God and world are "wholly other," absolutely dissimilar, then words whose meanings are drawn from the finite world are perhaps wholly inap-

plicable to God. If one's words are limited to the finite, then one cannot say anything about God positively, one can use only negations. Hence, according to the way of negation, it can be said that God is "not this, not that," but no more. The meaning of any finite word would be equivocal if applied to God.

It is obvious, however, that if God and world are not "wholly other," there may be some symbols that could be used of both God and world literally, or at least analogically. To insist on the *via negativa*, then, is to insist that God and world are absolutely dissimilar.

It should be mentioned that the "way of negation" is sometimes used differently, as when it is claimed by defenders of analogy that every analogy negates part of the literal meaning of the symbol used. The *via negativa* goes on to negate the entire meaning; it says "not at all like," rather than the "not exactly like" of analogy.

2. At the other extreme is what might be called the *via litera*, the way of literalness. Such a view would be championed by metaphysicians who hold that there are unitary characteristics extending throughout the whole of reality. Such a rule would be appropriate to a wide range of theories extending from certain forms of materialism to certain idealistic systems, from logical atomisms to theories stressing the interdependence of all things. What is required is merely that all things be modifications of the same substance, or share the same structure, or have certain basic characteristics in common.

3. In between is the way of analogy, an interpretation rule which requires that at least some basic metaphysical chacteristics be predicated analogically. Such a rule fits well the great-chain-of-being type of world in which there is a hierarchy of being such that, although there are certain characteristics which run throughout the hierarchy, these nevertheless vary from level to

level of the hierarchy. The word "life," it might be said, does not mean the same thing when predicated of an amoeba as it does when predicated of a man or when predicated of God. Nevertheless it means *similar* things, and the meaning of the word is not entirely different in these three cases. The usage, then, is neither univocal nor equivocal, it is analogical. It asserts both similarity and difference.

The great classical system of St. Thomas Aquinas was based on the notion that there are metaphysical characteristics of this sort. The *analogia entis*, analogy of being, was used to interpret the meaning of various categories which were held to extend throughout the whole order of being and to exist in ways appropriate to the various levels of being. The doctrine was held to be based on metaphysical proofs which showed that characteristics of finite being were present, in an analogous way, in God the creator of finite being.[12]

4. Conceivably one could reject all three ways introduced so far by claiming that there are certain objects known or relations entered into that cannot be symbolized literally or analogically (in the strict sense) but yet *can* be symbolized in some other way, thus avoiding the way of negation which denies that legitimate symbols can be found. One might argue, for example, that at times one finds oneself in relations which inevitably suggest certain symbols, and at the same time discover that one has no way of evaluating their accuracy since one has no access to the other term of the relation except through that relation. Some theists contend that certain symbols seem inevitable or appropriate for expressing the relation in which man stands to transcendence, and further state that man has no other access to transcendence besides these relations. Thus one cannot view transcendence nor can one prove that God's nature is analogous to the world. One can only stand in the relation and express

that relation in the words which inevitably arise. Or one might go on to claim that certain authorities guarantee the appropriateness of those symbols.

While it is rather easy to separate the rules, it is very difficult to know, often, whether a particular usage is literal or nonliteral and what kind of nonliteralness it might be. One reason for this is that, as Susanne Langer points out, language actually grows by means of metaphor or analogy. The claim that metaphysical method involves growth by means of metaphor has already been explored, indicating that there is a very close relationship between metaphysics building and language extension. Langer's point is that "every new experience, or new idea about things, evokes first of all some metaphorical expression. As the idea becomes familiar, this expression 'fades' to a new literal use of the once metaphorical predicate, a more general use than it had before." [13] In such a way, then, the literal meaning of terms is broadened as more and more experiences are symbolized by the same term; likewise a metaphysical system grows as the "root metaphor" is expanded into a world view.

Not all extensions, however, are retained, for two other fates may await the symbol. One may decide that the new case cannot really be treated in the same terms as the old; that is, one may decide that one has used what is sometimes called a "mere" metaphor or figure of speech. Or else it may happen that the metaphoric extension is retained *as metaphor* because the original situation and the new one are similar but not identical in their possession of the symbolized aspect.

Thus a metaphor may, on further investigation, be replaced by a new literal usage, remain a metaphor or analogy, or become a "mere" metaphor, depending upon what subsequent investigation yields. One must not, for that reason, conclude that a usage which is analogical as presently understood will always remain so.

There is another facet to this problem having to do with the preciseness with which a symbol is defined. Whether a particular usage is literal or nonliteral often depends upon the precise one of several related meanings which it is given in a specific case. If one chooses, for example, to define "person" in terms of human beings, then the use of the same symbol to refer to either God or lower animals would be at best analogical, at worst a "mere" metaphor. However, should one define "person" in terms merely of will and intellect, then the word might be used literally of God and of lower animals as well as of man.

It would be appropriate to some philosophers to hold that some or all analogies can be reduced to literal usages, as qualities which are merely accidental to the defining characteristics are dropped from the definition. For example, it has been argued that, since matter happens to accompany all instances of creation known to men, the literal meaning of "creation" includes reference to preexisting matter, and creation *ex nihilo* is an illegitimate expression. However, it seems quite clear that such a claim is highly arbitrary. The term "creation" can easily be abstracted from its normal setting as occurring-with-matter, and extended in usage to include creation *ex nihilo*. Thus occurring-with-matter would be dropped from the definition of creation, or, as it could be said, creation could be abstracted from occurring-with-matter.[14]

Such reduction in connotation might be very limited in usefulness, however, especially if those theologians and philosophers who hold that there are degrees of being are correct. In such a case there might be analogies which are irreducible.

One further complication must be mentioned. There may be literal usages and analogies which are perfectly valid and yet which are recognized as such by only a portion of humanity. Sometimes the validation of an analogy would require assuming a perspective which one cannot or will not take. Thus, that thinkers disagree as to the validity of a particular analogy, or as to literal usage, for that matter, does not necessarily prove anything more than that they disagree. It may indicate only that the validating perspective is lacking, and not that the analogy is invalid.

Reference has already been made to a kind of predication which is neither literal nor analogical but yet which *is* predication of some sort. The mode of predication is not literal because the object is known to be "other" than anything else man experiences and it is not analogical because it cannot be proved that this object has the qualities used to symbolize it, even in an analogous way. Dorothy Emmett asserts that religious symbols are of this sort. The only suitable test for religious symbols is "their appropriateness as expressions of response to something whose intrinsic nature cannot be apprehended in any direct way." She speaks also of whether or not the symbol "strikes us as an inevitable way of expressing a relation in which we stand to something of whose intrinsic nature we have no direct apprehension." [15]

Emmett gives her support to the view of religious symbols presented by Edwyn Bevan, who argues that the test for meaning in the case of religious symbols is a "pragmatic" one, whether such symbols "meet the exigencies of the human spirit" which is in tune with religious reality. When the theist asserts that God is Father he means to say that God is of such a character that "if any of us could know Him as He is (which we cannot do) and then had to describe in human language to men upon earth what he saw, he would have to say: 'What I see is undescribable, but if you think of God as a loving Father, I cannot put the Reality to you in a better way than that: that is the nearest you can get.'" [16]

One frequently encounters the claim that there are "insight" symbols of the above sort. H. F. Dunbar writes of symbols which provide a glimpse into a reality "completely beyond and beneath [the symbol] and imperceptible to sense *per se*." [17] The "insight" into the transcendent reality is provided by the occurrence of the symbol itself and cannot be tested by ordinary means.

Some rather unusual tests have been proposed, tests which would be quite appropriate for such symbols. The following have been suggested by Tillich, Wheelwright, and Urban, respectively: their "necessity for the symbol-creating consciousness"; whether "the believer, with his whole mind awake, receives an illumined conviction that it must be so"; and their authenticity "as valid expressions, for our type of consciousness, of the numinous quality of experience and its corresponding reference." [18] In addition, as has been mentioned, it is sometimes claimed that revelation is the source of such symbols, hence that they are authenticated by God Himself.

In the following chapter a number of questions concerning religious symbols will be considered; however, many of the arguments also have relevance to what might be called "non-religious" metaphysical views. Openness to the possibility that there are unusual rules for such symbols must be maintained, as indicated in the present chapter. It has been shown that different metaphysics imply different interpretation rules, and it has likewise been shown that different interpretation rules imply different metaphysics. One is certain of one's rules only when one is certain about one's world view and not vice versa, and even then one finds others equally certain about their rules and world views.

VI. Problems Concerning Symbols of Transcendence

———————◆◆◆————————

The preceding chapter contained explorations of general problems concerning the relationship of symbols to metaphysics and to things symbolized. Symbols of transcendence, usually called religious symbols, pose some special questions which will now be considered. Attention will be given to the alleged uniqueness of religious symbols, to problems of literal, analogical, and equivocal meaning as they relate to transcendence, and to the role of paradox, myth, and historical symbols in religion.

The Alleged Uniqueness of Religious Symbols

According to Paul Tillich, symbols are something more than mere signs and concepts. Their function is that of opening up levels of reality for which nonsymbolic language is inadequate. The symbol does not accomplish its task by merely picturing something; rather a symbol actually participates in the reality to which it points and makes that reality available to man. "This is the great function of symbols, to point beyond themselves in the power of that to which they point, to open up levels of reality which otherwise are closed, and to open up levels of the human mind of which we otherwise are not aware." [1] Thus they function as "insight" symbols, to use the term introduced in the previous chapter. Such symbols are not invented by thinking nor can they be abolished by thinking, but they are born out of a creative encounter with reality and last as long as the encounter lasts. Thus they cannot be replaced, for they themselves embody the insight which they present, and they embody it in an irreplaceable way.

Those who deal with religious symbols, such as theologians who reflect upon them, are bound by those which occur. Tillich states that "what theology can do with these symbols is to conceptualize them, to explain them, and to criticize them—these three things," but beyond this one cannot go. What criticism takes place is criticism in terms of other religious symbols, for nonsymbolic criticism of symbols is impossible. "If a symbol is criticized, it must be criticized within the bounds of symbolic meaning. We must criticize it from the inside, comparing elements of it with the whole of the symbolic system to which they belong." [2] Thus theology is bound by the symbols which it analyzes, and cannot replace such symbols by neutral philosophical concepts.

Tillich means something beyond the usual sense in which symbols might be said to be irreplaceable. A flag, for instance, symbolizes a nation uniquely, but it could be largely replaced by concepts and other symbols. However, he argues, religious symbols cannot at all be replaced by concepts, nor can they be destroyed through theoretical criticism. He asserts that "it is not theoretical criticism which kills religious symbols, but rather a change in the actual encounter," going on to claim that religious symbols are "not on a level on which empirical criticism can dismiss them," for "their truth is their adequacy to the religious system in which they are created, and their inadequacy to another situation is their untruth." [3] Thus the adequacy of religious symbols is tested by their inevitability as expressions of a particular encounter with transcendence, and by no other way. It is tested in terms of a system of symbols and apparently not in terms of a reality which transcends that system, so his language seems to suggest.

This claim of Tillich's is misleading. Changes in symbols are related to changes in metaphysical views. His claim is that Protestant theology rejected the "virgin birth" symbol not because it is of secondary importance in Scripture, not because of historical research or scientific theories, but because the doctrine of virgin birth "takes away one of the fundamental doctrines of Chalcedon," namely the doctrine of the full humanity of Christ.[4] Tillich's thesis seems to require that the view has changed because finally, after all these centuries, the implications of the Chalcedonian symbols were worked out and the intra-systematic contradiction between Chalcedonian symbols and the virgin birth symbol was realized. However, it is surely more plausible to argue that the emergence of a radically different world view had some effect on the changed attitude toward the virgin birth. One would suppose that scientific and philosophical skepticism about miracles had at least something to do with it.

In fact, it would seem to be evident that the particular view of the nature of religious language which Tillich offers is itself the product of a basic change in world view from that of classical Christianity. Tillich is offering a view of religious symbols which has been made necessary by a rejection of the metaphysics underlying both the biblical and the classical religious traditions and which would have been rejected by both biblical and classical Christianity. While it is true that symbolic interpretation of Christian symbols has been accepted throughout Christian history, *the literal truth of these symbols was also defended*, and traditional theologians unquestionably took their claims to be factual in the metaphysical sense of that word, defending their claims by use of science and reason. It seems far-fetched to say that "the gods of polytheism did not disappear through philosophical criticism; rather they could be successfully criticized philosophically only *after* the encounter out of which they were born already had ceased to be."[5] Philosophical criticism was quite relevant; so at least the accusers of Socrates felt.

When Edwyn Bevan points out that there are *two* ways by which religious symbols are rejected, he is more correct than Tillich, but even Bevan puts the emphasis in the wrong place. The usual reason, he says, is that such symbols "are displaced by some other positive conception which meets the spiritual exigence better than the previous one," but he also admits that sometimes they are rejected "because something in them is shown by rational criticism to be incompatible with our general beliefs about the universe."[6] That symbols of God change as metaphysical and scientific views change implies that there *is* a relationship between the two, that theologies in the past have not been independent of metaphysical views, and that adequacy to the religious encounter is not the sole criterion for evaluating religious symbols. Hence religious symbols are not absolutely independent of metaphysical criticism. Whatever uniqueness they have arises from the kind of reality which they symbolize, and not from their exemption from philosophical scrutiny.

Literal, Analogical, Equivocal, and Nondescriptively Analogical Symbols

It was suggested in the preceding chapter that how a word means, whether its meaning in specific cases is literal or analogical, is often a function of the breadth of the definition which is being used. A minimal definition, it would seem evident, enables one in include more within the class formed by that definition, thus allowing for a wider literal signification, than a maximal definition. The more specific characteristics included in a definition, the narrower would be its literal extent and vice versa. Thus the class of red objects is broader than the class of red squares, broader still than the class of rough-textured red squares, and so on. A usage which would be literal when a single characteristic is the basis for classification might be metaphorical were several characteristics included in the definition.

The following statements might be said to be used literally or analogically or equivocally depending upon what the assertions are taken to mean, depending upon how specifically the concepts are defined. The statements "God is our father," "God is a person," and "God exists" can each be understood in several ways.

A. Literal. If what is meant by "God is our father" is merely that God is the source from which man proceeds, man's cause, as it would normally be taken to mean since few sophisticated persons would think of God as literally a big daddy, then the statement can be treated as literal so long as it is remembered that nothing more than this causative relation is affirmed. Thus also one would speak of being father of an idea, or of an amoeba's being father to its offspring, both usages being confirmed by standard dictionary definitions of "father."

Although normally it would be said that these are analogical, not literal, usages, it would be meaningful to claim that the usage is univocal provided that by being father is meant merely what is specified above. It is not normally said, for example, that "two" is used literally when describing each of two pairs of apples but analogically when used to describe a pair of apples and twins, for here one is used to the fact that two refers to a single characteristic and no more. "To the left of" is used literally of both planets and books. Why should "being father of" be intrinsically less literal when applied to different kinds of things?

Robert L. Calhoun has argued for the legitimacy of the use of "person" for God since "personality is not of a certain size, like a physical body; though, for that matter, no certain size can be specified as the 'summit' for animal bodies. . . . In any event, mind and personality are pervasive, not localized characteristics; more like life than like a particular organ or a physical frame." [7] A number of philosophers and theologians, including E. S. Brightman, Charles Hartshorne, Nels Ferre, and Emil Brunner, as well as many lesser known modern figures, have adopted similar positions. However, there are also theologians who would object to the suitability of this term *however* defined, holding that God transcends the category of personality.

Similarly, that God exists could be affirmed as literally true, given a suitably defined meaning for that troublesome word. If by "exist" were meant "manifests itself in space and time" when "in" does not necessarily mean location in some specific, restricted area of space but could include being coterminous with space, then God could be said to exist according to some religious views. One might want to point out that things which exist have many characteristics which set them apart from one another. Just as amoebas are fathers by fission, humans by generation, and God by creating *ex nihilo* perhaps, there may be suitable distinctions among beings that manifest themselves in space and time. Possibly the most suitable distinction would be that between beings that come into being and pass away and beings that do not, or, to use more customary language, finite beings and Infinite beings.[8]

Tillich's objection to the expression "God exists" seems mistaken. His claim is that to speak of God as existing implies "that God is a being, acting in time and space, dwelling in a special place, affecting the course of events and being affected by them like any other being in the universe." [9] Classical theologians

would have denied that this was implied, and there seems to be
no good reason for admitting Tillich's claim. To say that an
object exists is not *necessarily* to say that it is a being like all
others. It might, for example, be an all-inclusive being and therefore quite different from non-all-inclusive beings. Or it might
have other qualities quite different from those of other existing
beings.

B. Analogical. Were more concrete content introduced into
the definitions, these other usages would become clearly analogical. Thus if fatherhood is defined specifically in terms of human
parenthood, then to speak either of an amoeba as father or of
God as father would be to speak analogically. The more qualities that are contained in the definition, the more restricted
becomes its literal application, and, were this process carried to
its conclusion, it would lead to the assertion that the second use
of every word is analogical. This would be true because, as was
said of old, one cannot step into the same river twice, since no
river is exactly the same again. Therefore, if a word were to
refer to the whole circumstance of a thing, it could never be used
again in a literal sense. Fortunately, words are not used this way
because they are used for abstractions from concrete fullness;
hence they are useful repeatedly, but at the price of fullness.
When the process is carried fully to the opposite extreme, the
barest abstractions are asserted with almost nothing of concrete
fullness being included. The barer the abstraction the greater
its literal extent, the richer the definition the greater its analogical
extent.

Certain traditions would deny emphatically that predicates can
be applied univocally to God and man. Eric Mascall claims that
"having satisfied ourselves that the existence of finite being
declares its dependence upon self-existent being, we then apprehend that no predicate can be attributed to finite and to self-

existent being univocally." [10] The conviction here is that infinite being is qualitatively different from finite being. If this conviction is correct, then basic metaphysical categories must be non-literal; however, if it is not correct, then there is a possibility that the basic categories could be used literally.

The great classical tradition in Western thought has followed the way of analogy, or sometimes the way of negation, and has denied that religious symbols can be predicated literally of both God and world. It must be pointed out, however, that this notion was closely tied to the philosophical view that there are degrees of reality, a view which has increasingly come under metaphysical attack. If reality has no degrees, then basic categories may well be literal.

C. Equivocal. Were one to go further by denying that qualities shared in by finite beings could in any sense be attributed to God, then all religious symbols would be equivocal in their application to God. Thus anyone who holds that God is literally Wholly Other would seemingly be forced to assert that religious symbols have no descriptive meaning. Such a stand is taken by W. T. Stace in his books on mysticism when he claims that religious symbols cannot in any sense *describe* God, they can only evoke experiences of God.

Stace's claim is that if the Otherness of God explicitly stated in much religious language is to be taken really seriously, then some rather radical consequences for theology result, for theologians must reject *all* predicates whether negative or positive. His reason for excluding all predicates is that "if there is a resemblance between the natural character which is here used as a symbol and the supernatural reality which it symbolizes, then there is a common element as between the two, and therefore the possibility of a concept." [11] If God is Wholly Other, then there are no elements in common between God and finite reality;

hence no words from the latter realm can be applied to the former. If God is Wholly Other, then words used for Him must mean something wholly other than what they normally do.

If God is really Wholly Other, Absolute, Infinite, and Changeless, as classical theologians typically said, then it would be inconsistent to affirm predicates which in any sense implied relatedness to the world. Stace then points to something which he claims makes that tradition inconsistent, its assertion that the existence of God could be proved from His relation to the world as First Cause. "If God is related to other things as their cause, then He is finite, since the otherness of these other things limits His being." [12] Moreover, finiteness would also be implied by any affirmation that God is mind, love, or person in any sense of those words. Either one must affirm the Otherness of God and deny relatedness or he must affirm relatedness and deny the Otherness of God. However, Stace claims, one cannot do both things at the same time as the classical tradition has done.[13]

Although Stace rather curiously omits consideration in depth of the classical doctrine of analogy, his arguments would still stand had he examined that tradition, for one cannot turn relatedness into absence of relation by intensifying it. If love involves relation, then greater love would seem to involve greater relation. If knowledge involves relation, then higher knowledge would involve greater relation, and so on. Thus the doctrine of analogy does not seem to offer classical theology an escape from the dilemma.

Perhaps, however, a different conclusion ought to be drawn from this inconsistency. Perhaps one should conclude that God ought not to be thought of as Wholly Other. Stace acknowledges that there are certain religious symbols which are used recurringly, but insists that those symbols in no sense describe God.

When a religious genius speaks, "our spirits vibrate faintly in unison with the soul of the great mystic, as a tuning fork vibrates faintly in response to the sound of the clear bell. But it is our own spontaneous experience which is evoked; it is not his experience which is communicated to us." [14] Thus religious symbols do not describe God but merely evoke experiences in those to whom the symbols speak.

The question then arises as to how it can be that certain words seem to evoke religious experience while other words do not, unless there is some degree of resemblance between what the word means and what the experience is. The word "love" is typically used by mystics, whereas "hate" is not. Words connoting supreme happiness are typically used while words connoting misery are not. There must be some explanation for this pattern other than mere happenstance. The only explanation that makes real sense is that certain symbols more nearly describe God than others do; hence those symbols recur and the others do not. Since words importing relation are among those that recur, then these words must in some sense describe God and He cannot be *Wholly* Other. The same claim would apply to words denying relation, with the same conclusion. If the words are useful, then God cannot be literally Wholly *Other*.

D. Nondescriptive analogies. There is another way of interpreting religious symbols which seeks to avoid both the assertion that religious symbols are literal or that they are analogical and the assertion that religious symbols are nondescriptive. It was indicated in the preceding chapter that some thinkers maintain an agnosticism as to God's nature while affirming that religious symbols do have a descriptive function and are subject to testing. Such is the case if religious symbols describe not God's nature but the relation in which man stands to transcendence.

Dorothy Emmett, in advancing such a view, says that we must ask of religious symbols "whether they are expressing the character of some actual *relation*." "The question is whether such a symbol strikes us as an inevitable way of expressing a relation in which we stand." [15] However, she insists that God's nature cannot be directly apprehended; what is apprehended is merely the relation in which man stands to God.

There is an inconsistency here, however, because if Emmett has warrant for asserting that man is related to God, and that such symbols as Father, Spirit, love are appropriate to describe this relation, then surely she has said something about God's nature and cannot be agnostic about it. She has said that God is the kind of being who stands in a relation to man which can appropriately be called "fatherly" or "loving."

The price of affirming real relation is the further affirmation that transcendence is related: the price of denying real relation is the further denial that man knows really that he is related to anything. In the latter case he would have to admit that he is perhaps only describing his subjective mental states when he uses religious symbols, and not referring to anything Beyond at all.

This point is illustrated further in Martin Buber's treatment of religious symbols, a view which Emmett notes with favor. Buber claims also that symbols point not to God but rather to man's relation to God. When man and God stand face to face, "man receives, and he receives not a specific 'content' but a Presence," and, as Buber goes on to say, "we acquire no knowledge from it." [16] What happens is that man enters into a relation, but in this relation he receives knowledge only about the relation, not about the God who is at the other end of the relation. When Buber speaks of God as the Eternal Thou he means that our relationship with him is eternally the I-Thou relation, not that God is in Himself a Thou.

But such a position seems untenable. The existence of such relations to God must give knowledge of a sort as to the nature of God, namely, that God is a being to whom man can be related. Sometimes Buber seems to admit this. An examination of the following passages indicates both Buber's refusal to allow that there is knowledge of God and his tacit admission that such knowledge is possible. In speaking of man's relation to God, he says: "This presupposes the existence of a Being, who, though in himself unlimited and unconditioned, lets other beings, limited and conditioned indeed, exist outside Himself. He even allows them to enter into a relation with Himslf such as seemingly can only exist between limited and conditioned beings. . . . In the reality of the religious relation the Absolute becomes in most cases personal." He hastens to add that "in so doing we are making no statement about the Absolute which reduces it to the personal. We are rather saying that it enters into the relationship as the Absolute Person whom we call God." [17]

Shunting aside the question as to whether speaking of God as personal is a reduction, a statement which ought to be questioned, it certainly seems that Buber is affirming many things about God's nature. He avoids saying that God is personal, but does say that God is the sort of being who can become personal. One might want to argue that a being who can decide to enter into personal relations with men must *be* personal; however, this objection aside, to say that God is the sort of being who can become personal is to convey important knowledge about the nature of God.

The following statements also contain implications about the Divine nature. Buber states, for example, that "you know always in your heart that you need God more than anything; but do you not know too that God needs you—in the fullness of His eternity needs you?" Then he goes on to say that man would not even be if God did not need him. Elaborating further, although speaking also of turgid and presumptuous talk about the "God who becomes," he says that "we know unshakably in our hearts that there is a becoming of the God that is. The world is not divine sport, it is divine destiny. There is divine meaning in the life of the world, of man, of human persons, of you and of me." [18] This statement contains many assertions about the nature of God even though it does not supply concepts for describing that nature.

Thus the attempt to maintain that man stands in real relation to God but that he has no knowledge of the Divine nature fails. If the relation is real, then man has knowledge of God; if it is not real, then man does not stand in that relation and is merely speaking about himself when he uses religious symbols.

The foregoing remarks do not prove that either literal or analogical knowledge of God is possible, but merely show that claiming to define the suitability of religious symbols in terms of man's relation to God while remaining totally agnostic about God's nature is untenable. One may either be totally agnostic about God's nature and deny that legitimate religious symbols are possible, or else affirm some knowledge of God's nature, thus providing for the possibility of religious symbols.

Analogy and Paradox

To use an analogy is to assert a similarity or resemblance between two things; however, it must be remembered that *only* a similarity or resemblance is being asserted. If there is more than a similarity, if the two things are identical, then the analogy passes over into a literal usage. The interpretation of an analogy, therefore, involves both affirmation and negation of the literal meaning of the term used, both the application of some quality or character and the denial of its complete applicability.

If one were to define "person" in such a way that it denotes only human beings, then to describe God as a person would be to use an analogy, the interpretation of which requires both affirmation and negation. One would be asserting that there is in God something like that quality symbolized by the word "person," but in addition one would be asserting that there is merely a likeness, not an exact sameness. The following rule, then, must be applied to all cases of genuine analogy: "We speak affirmatively and negatively of God at the same time, asserting the image as genuinely revealing while denying the limitations which our experience of it inevitably suggests." [19]

Since this is the character of analogical predication it is difficult to describe disagreement between analogies accurately. Of two literal statements one may say that when a statement affirms a certain character of something and another statement denies that character, then the two statements contradict, and one statement at most can be correct. With analogies the matter is not that simple, for analogies assert similarities, but they also assert differences at the same time; hence it is difficult to conceive of two analogies strictly contradicting one another. Strictly speaking, to contradict an analogy would be to claim that there is no similarity of the required sort; merely to assert a competing analogy would not be sufficient.

Statements which would be contradictory when viewed literally are not contradictory as analogies. To say, for example, that God is personal (analogically) but that God is not a person (literally) would involve no contradiction. Rather, the second statement would be merely an explication of the meaning of the first. Similarity with "God is person" and "God is not person" when both are analogical assertions, the one merely asserts that God is in some sense personal, while the other asserts that in some sense He is not personal, and the two statements together explicate the meaning of saying that the symbol "person" is used analogically when applied to God.

Sometimes this point is overlooked and this inescapable feature of analogical predication is turned into something else, into "paradox." Donald Baillie has spoken of the need for paradox in theological discourse, meaning by paradox the affirmation of "two contradictory, logically incompatible but ontologically necessary assertions" as both true.[20] Whether or not there are such cases, the example which he uses to illustrate his claim fails to establish it. Baillie cites as his example the need for using two different kinds of flat maps to depict spherical surfaces, a map which takes the form of two hemispheres, and a flat, oblong, Mercator projection. His claim is that these two types of map contradict each other at every point, and yet both kinds must be used to convey correctly spherical relationships.

The difficulty with the example is that in this case the maps are not really mutually contradictory. The rules by which the two kinds of maps are interpreted *preclude* their being taken in a contradictory way, for the maps result from different kinds of projection and are read accordingly. Both maps are distortions, and the distorting rules are known; together they work in a complementary, not in a contradictory, manner. Were the maps literal, then the two maps would be contradictory. It is the fact that they are not, that they are analogical representations, that saves them from flat contradiction.

There are other uses of language involving simultaneous affirmation and denial which could be called paradoxes only in this weak sense. Many times striking verbal expressions are spoken of as paradoxical, expressions which can be replaced by statements having no appearance of being paradoxical. The "paradox" of having to lose one's life in order to find it is one example of such. Or, ideas which are new and contrary to the usual ways of looking at things, which are "against the opinion," to use the root meaning of the word "paradox," are sometimes called paradoxical. In this sense it was paradoxical for a while to think of the earth as moving about the sun, and paradoxical to think of two straight lines which cross a transversal such that the alternate interior angles are equal as meeting, but with familiarity this sort of paradox is dissolved.

Of paradox in the strong sense, paradox as the assertion of two contradictory, logically incompatible propositions, several things must be said. First, a distinction ought to be made between paradoxes of thought and paradoxes of being, such that one might hold that paradoxes of thought may occur about things which are in themselves unparadoxical. The example often cited is the use of both wave and particle theories for interpreting the behavior of light. In such cases, however, one would usually say that the fault, dear Brutus, is in ourselves, that our categories are inadequate to describe the thing.

It is difficult to imagine what it would be like for reality itself to be self-contradictory. Some would say that it is logically impossible for reality to be self-contradictory or paradoxical, hence that it is possible to rule out *a priori* paradoxes of being. Others would say merely that "we could not say of any 'unlogical' world how it would look," indicating merely our inability to think in such terms. Whichever the conclusion one draws, the point is a good one, and it seems to be the case that few thinkers really carry the case for paradox to reality itself.

Paradoxes of thought can often be resolved, and some philosophers would assert that such is the case with the standard theological paradoxes. Charles Hartshorne has devoted much

effort to the attempt to show that an unparadoxical concept of
God can be achieved. His claim is that predicates which import
the relativity of God can be applied to God's concrete being,
whereas predicates importing absoluteness can be applied to
God's essential nature or structure or abstract Essence, without
there being any contradiction since the affirmations are applied
to different aspects of God.[21] A. C. Knudson suggests that
identity and change as well as unity and diversity can be related
unparadoxically by means of the concept "person." "A person
is one. He knows himself to be such. Yet he does many different things. . . . In a similar way he is conscious of his own
identity. He knows that he is the same 'I,' the same person he
was a year ago or fifty years ago. Yet he has in many respects
changed during these years." [22] Joseph Katz and others have
argued that the paradox of time and eternity can also be resolved through a reversal of the usual relationship. Katz suggests that although time cannot be unparadoxically contained
in eternity, eternity can be conceived in terms of time, as "an
aspect of *temporal* reality—primarily that aspect which is char-
acterized by such attributes as rest, stability, and unity." [23] Some
able scholars have concluded that the biblical notion of eternity's
relation to time was nonparadoxical. Edwyn Bevan claims that
the notion of eternity as something wholly different from time
infiltrated Christian thought from Neoplatonic sources and that
"so far as the language of the Bible goes, there is nothing to
show that the eternity of God is understood in any other sense
than that of unending time." [24]

    There are those, perhaps, who would reject both the proposed
resolution of these paradoxes and the claim that paradoxes are
paradoxes of language only, but even Soren Kierkegaard, the
arch-theologian of paradox, seemingly says merely that God is
paradoxical *for us* and not in Himself. He states in several places

that for God reality is a system, and that there is conformity between thought and being for God, but not for us.[25] This implies that paradoxes are paradoxes of thought, not of being. However, Kierkegaard would never assent to the claim that these paradoxes of thought are subject to resolution through reformulation of the problem. Instead, for him, careful analysis of the problem merely heightens the paradox and serves to indicate more clearly the radical difference between God and man. It is man's finiteness, not God's being, that makes paradox inevitable.

Myths and Historical Symbols

The word "myth" has a multiplicity of meanings, many of which are irrelevant to this inquiry. Sometimes the word is used to mean that which is fictitious and sometimes it is used to designate a particular way of organizing reality which is opposed to scientific or logical orderings. A third definition is the one which is used here. Tillich claims that the original meaning of the Greek word "mythos" has to do with "stories of the gods," and goes on to add that "this is the world of the myth . . . man's ultimate concern symbolized in divine figures and actions. Myths are symbols of faith combined in stories about divine human encounters." [26] Rudolf Bultmann's definition is similar: mythology is the "use of imagery to express the otherworldly in terms of this world and the divine in terms of human life, the other side in terms of this side." [27] For both Bultmann and Tillich this means that mythology is *ipso facto* inadequate, because God cannot be described in such terms; but this is a claim which requires proof, for if the divine is something which *can* be expressed in terms drawn from this world then some myths at least may be literally true.

It is unlikely that anyone would defend all myths, for every kind of object and being has been used at some time or another in myths and there is often much in myth that is sheer fantasy. What is being discussed here is not whether every myth is adequate, but whether the mythical category can be used to depict the Divine being; in short, whether myth can be a sophisticated philosophical and religious category.

The adequacy of myth depends upon the nature of the Divine. Perhaps myths need some interpretation, but it is not clear that mythology can be eliminated categorically, particularly not if, as Casserley has claimed, "truth cannot be told without myth because reality is drama rather than process." [28] There are those who hold that God is "*a* Being, not Being-Itself" and who argue that a "bold anthropomorphism" is the only adequate way to speak about God,[29] whereas others would completely reject the adequacy of such language, insisting that all myths must be "broken" or transcended. In between these two positions there are those who might use personal symbols analogically.

There is another kind of symbol which is much in vogue in contemporary theology, the historical symbol. An historical symbol is one which asserts that particular historical events symbolize the Divine. Such symbols are to be contrasted with symbols which have no special temporal reference but are timeless or else refer to all times equally.

Biblical theologians often point to the historical symbol as being of crucial significance, arguing that man has no access to God except through his revelation in special historical events. Cherbonnier, defending what he claims to be the biblical philosophy, argues that "God himself is a protagonist in the drama of history, a real-life drama in which man's salvation is won and lost, here and now." [30] Similarly, Emil Brunner claims that "Christian faith is faith in the historical revelation and redemption; faith in the redeeming, revealing intervention of God in history; faith in a definite, unique, unexchangeable, divine history." [31] Both would claim that man cannot really know God's existence or nature apart from this revelation of God in history, and both would hold that a philosophical view of God can be built upon this revelation. Hence, particular historic events reveal God's nature, and historical symbols are needed to refer to those events.

Traditional Christian theology and classical philosophy tended to subordinate the historical symbol to timeless ones. Typical classical discussions of the existence and nature of God move from proofs for God's existence to discussions of His nature in terms of timeless categories such as infinity, changelessness, and so on, and only then, if at all, to categories suggested by historical symbols. However, historical symbols are more likely to be used by some more recent theological traditions. H. Richard Niebuhr's classic work on revelation stresses as its central theme the inescapable partnership between Christianity and history. "When we speak of revelation we mean that something has happened to us in our history which conditions all our thinking and that through this happening we are enabled to apprehend what we are, what we are suffering and doing and what our potentialities are." [32] For Christianity this something is the revelation of God in the person of Jesus of Nazareth, an event which can be located in space and time at least as far as its external aspects are concerned. Although there is more to the event than can be discerned by the secular historian, the event has an external and objective aspect in a special historical time and place.

Similarly, Cherbonnier suggests that religious symbols are necessarily historical because God is a God who acts in particular moments in history, and whose nature is to be understood in terms of the particular events in which He has acted. It is certainly an oversimplification to claim, as he does, that the adequacy of biblical philosophy can be proved by simple reference to the facts of history. His claim is, correctly, that the truth of historical "symbols is wholly dependent upon the factuality of the events which they symbolize," but it is hardly justifiable to say that those who reject this God "can be refuted by objective evidence" because "Biblical theology does acknowledge objective standards of verification, both logical and factual." [33] Such a claim seems to imply that non-Christians are making simple factual and logical mistakes when they reject Christianity, that they are denying obvious and easily verified historical facts. This is surely an oversimplification, as Cherbonnier seems to recognize at times.

Basic disagreements in metaphysics cannot be settled so simply since the presence of different views is itself evidence of an absence of agreement as to what the facts are. Appeals to history, to past and present "facts," are appeals to metaphysized history, as people actually make them, and not to "plain facts."

An individual symbol is an implicit metaphysical system in that it has its place in linguistic and other contexts which enter into its very meaning. A metaphysical system is a total symbol or system of symbols. The truth of a metaphysical system is established, in part, through a careful comparison of its symbols with reality, but it is also the case that the adequacy of individual symbols and groups of symbols is established, in part, through metaphysical thinking, through the development of a total understanding of reality.

Hence one does not begin the task of philosophizing with some body of tested and true symbolic rules, criteria of truth, canons of factuality and logicality; one discovers what these are as one pursues the task of metaphysics building, at the end of the quest, not at the beginning. Not all metaphysicians discover the same things, as the perennial character of basic metaphysical disputes abundantly indicates.

Some attention has been given in these chapters on symbols to the various types of symbols and the requirements for their interpretation, particularly as regards their relativity to specific metaphysical views or groups of views. Questions as to whether metaphysical views must be literal or analogical or metaphorical in some additional sense, whether or not views can be non-paradoxical, whether myths and historical symbols are necessary or dispensable, all these questions must be left open as live possibilities since various metaphysical answers require differing theories. The quest for an adequate metaphysical description of reality is at the same time the quest for an adequate symbolism; the solution to the two problems is the same.

In the chapters which remain, attention will be given to the question of the proof of metaphysical theories, for metaphysical theories in general and for theistic metaphysics in particular.

Summary

It has been argued that religious symbols are not different from any other symbols by being exempt from metaphysical criticism. Any differences have merely to do with the reality they describe. The evidence cited was the fact that the interpretation of religious symbols does seem to be affected by scientific and rational criticism.

Secondly, it has been pointed out that sometimes the type of meaning which a symbol has is a function of the degree of specificity of its definition. Moreover, if the classical doctrine of degrees of being is in error, it is possible that many religious symbols can be interpreted literally. In addition, the claim has been made that if God is Wholly Other, then religious symbols have no descriptive function. Conversely, if religious symbols have a descriptive function, then God cannot be Wholly Other. The claim was then advanced that the position is untenable which holds that religious symbols do not describe God or give clues as to His nature because they merely describe man's relation to God. If the relation is real, then something is known about God's nature. Conversely, if nothing is known about God's nature, then the relation cannot be said to be real.

Thirdly, it has been noted that the use of the method of analogy implies the use of paradox, in the weak sense of that word. Certain difficulties involved in the claim that analogies can be contradictory were pointed out. It was also noted that the fact that paradoxes of thought may be necessary, temporarily or perhaps permanently, need not indicate that reality is paradoxical in the strong sense of that word.

Lastly, the adequacy of myth and historical symbols for certain types of doctrine of God has been noted. These categories cannot be rejected *a priori,* for to do so would be to beg the metaphysical question of the nature of God. To assume that myth is inadequate would be to eliminate an important philosophical tradition arbitrarily.

VII. Theism and Metaphysical Proof

Metaphysical descriptions, because they are total descriptions, must take into consideration the whole of man's experience and symbolic activities, and this includes his religious activities and symbols. Therefore metaphysics must attempt to "do justice to" man's religious symbols. A metaphysic, to be adequate, must furnish some explanation for the origin and persistence of theism and other forms of religion, and this involves providing some sensible explanation as to why reasonable men both are religious and remain religious in the face of critical attacks. This explanation might take the form of a "reduction" of religious assertions to some noncognitive status or it might take the form of creating and defending a full-blown theistic world view, but some serious account of religion must be provided if a world view is to prove to be adequate. To assume, or to smuggle in by means of assumptions as to what the facts are or as to what the proper logical rules are, either theism or nontheism would be an arbitrary procedure. Hence the attempt has been made throughout this inquiry to leave the various logical alternatives open and, since theism is one of these possibilities, to arrive at analyses which would allow for the statement of the theistic case.

Theism, however, obviously has a peculiar status when compared with many other metaphysical alternatives. Its status is unusual because the things which theism appeals to are not as tangible or obvious to everyone as those things to which some other world views can appeal. Thus, however true it is to say that theism is a metaphysical possibility alongside others, it must also be said that validating its claims is a relatively complicated undertaking. While naturalism has only the problems of fitting its theoretical descriptions to a reality which everyone more or less acknowledges, theism has to show that it is dealing with something real when it speaks of God. For naturalism, the problem is merely that of showing how an obvious reality is to be described, while theism has the additional problem of showing that it is talking about something beyond the human mind and its constructs.

One might demur at this point by claiming that naturalism must also provide an explanation for the existence of the reality it describes, thus must raise questions of ultimate purpose and causation, but that this is so is not clear. There is no *a priori* reason why reality *must* depend upon something prior to itself for its existence. Only theists and other defenders of religion seem to feel that there is any need to postulate a first cause, and it is difficult to show that an idea is self-evident which is rejected as not self-evident by a sizable number of philosophers, some of them religious. St. Thomas Aquinas himself denied that reason could prove a first cause in time, and his own form of cosmological argument, related to the alleged dependence of the contingent order on some Necessary Being, is not widely accepted outside theistic circles, and is ofttimes rejected within theistic circles.

Naturalism can make its case in terms of experiences accessible to everyone, and experiences which everyone admits that he has. Theism cannot, for however much some theists may argue that everyone *really* experiences God, the testimony of many naturalists is that they do not. And even were the theistic case granted at this point, all that it would logically imply is that everyone has experiences of finiteness or has religious experiences, and not that the religious *interpretation* of these experiences is the one which ought to be given. Whereas everyone would agree, at least roughly, as to what interpretation ought to be given to the kind of sense experiences with which naturalists are concerned.

Everyone admits, roughly speaking, that events are subject to naturalistic explanations, that experiences resembling religious ones can be produced by drugs or can be hallucinated without them. Not everyone admits the interpretation that theism makes, namely, that there are also veridical elements to these experiences. Thus theism has the harder case wherever one looks, unless one appeals merely to the question of ease or naturalness of belief, in which case theism perhaps has had the edge, at least up to now. However, since ease of belief is a psychological criterion, appeal to it cannot really decide basic metaphysical questions.

The problem for theism is thus that of communicating some perspective upon reality which justifies going beyond naturalism, and in order to do this the theistic philosopher must communicate two things: what he sees that goes beyond naturalism; and his reason for supposing that what he sees is true. To be able to test theism one must know what the theist says and one must know why he thinks that he must say it.

The theistic point of view *can* be communicated to an extent, for theists and nontheists both know, at least vaguely, what is being talked about when the claim is made that God exists. They may argue about whether there is really any evidence to support the claim that God exists, but they know the sort of thing that is being claimed. It is now fashionable to say that the logical peculiarities of theistic assertions, the ways in which theistic language is used, indicate the sort of thing that is meant.

Moreover, both theists and nontheists are aware of the types of things which constitute difficulties for theism, thus indicating that both sides are aware of what theism is claiming. Both sides are also aware of the experiences known as religious and the arguments which are regarded as proofs for God's existence, as well as the "contingency" of which Neo-Thomists make so much. They agree on the "plain facts," in short, but disagree as to how these facts should be seen, as to what should be read into (or out of) the facts, and as to what conclusions should be derived from them.

It is also clear that it is possible to understand, more or less, what ought to be the case were theism true. For example, as John Hick has observed, "religious people claim to apprehend God by faith, and epistemological investigation should be able to indicate whether the kind of cognition claimed is such as might reasonably be expected to occur if there is indeed a God to be known." [1] It ought to be possible, in principle, to explicate the whole logic of any metaphysical position in order to indicate the features of the system, and to indicate at least vaguely what view one would have to take were the position true.

The Status of Theistic Assertions

The fact that people do argue intelligently about the truth of theism itself indicates that theism is a meaningful metaphysical alternative. It would also seem to indicate that the theistic world view can be treated as one metaphysical hypothesis alongside others. Theological objections to considering theism as hypothetical have already been considered and rejected on several grounds. Theistic assertions do change and they are regarded as being subject to doubt. Besides, even if beliefs were held with absolute certainty this would indicate merely something about the way in which they were held, not something about their truth, since false ideas can be held with certainty. Once "certain" doctrines prove false, as some have, then the method of absolute certainty is suspect.

There are, however, other objections to considering theistic assertions as hypotheses which must now be considered. The first of these is based on the claim that theism can be proved and that it therefore has a truth status beyond the probability usually assigned to hypotheses.

To review the literature on the proofs for the existence of God is unnecessary, and some claims for such proofs have already received attention. The arguments, as formulated by Neo-Thomists, proceed from an awareness of the finiteness of being to the intellectual judgment that such being is effect-implying-cause. It is rather obvious that nontheists seem to have the requisite experience, as is amply illustrated in atheistic forms of existentialism, but they do not find themselves forced to acknowledge that their being implies a cause which is other than another finite form of being.

The ontological argument rests, most philosophers aver, on logical fallacies, and this comment holds even for modern revisions of the argument. The teleological argument runs afoul of the problem of evil, and is at best inconclusive because of the signs of apparent disorder in the universe, and because non-teleological explanations for many "purposive" features of man can be supplied. Even if valid, the argument enables one to conclude only that there is probably a God, if it be granted that empirical arguments yield only probable conclusions; hence it would not be the kind of firm logical proof which would take the existence of God beyond the realm of hypothesis.

There is another sort of objection to speaking of theistic assertions as hypotheses. It is sometimes said that the assertion that God exists is not based on inductive inference, nor is it a probable hypothesis in the usual sense of the word; hence it is not really suitable to speak of such a view as a hypothesis. Ordinarily, hypotheses are subject to some sort of verification in terms of an appeal to evidence which would tend to decide the matter one way or the other. This is not the case with theism, since all the evidences it points to are ambiguous. Moreover, so the objection runs, the reasoning which is alleged to lead to God's existence is different from ordinary cases of inference, even analogical inference. Ordinarily one might, on meeting a lion, infer that the lion is tame, the basis for the inference being that one has observed both wild lions and tame ones and has learned from many examples what behavior characterizes each. However, in the case of the world of ordinary experience, the problem obviously is different. There are not *many* worlds to experience, some created and some uncreated; therefore one does not have the opportunity to study carefully the kinds of characteristics which each type of world has. All that seems to be available for metaphysics is one world, and whether it is an example of a created world or an uncreated world is precisely the point at issue.

Nevertheless, despite these pecularities it is justifiable to speak of the existence of God as a matter of legitimate speculation. Even though it is true that the whole world cannot be experienced and judgments as to its nature drawn on the basis of such experience, and even though it is true that there is a paucity of worlds available for examination, it is nevertheless reasonable to conjecture as to whether the world is created or not, and to elaborate that conjecture into a world view for testing. Human beings have had considerable experience of portions of the world and of objects that have been fashioned by human beings, and on the basis of that limited experience have the legitimate right to speculate as to whether that portion of the world which they see is more like the created objects in their experience than like the ones which do not seem to have been designed, more like artistic creations and mathematical models than matters of mere happenstance.

Again, that theism is a legitimate hypothesis is indicated by the fact that people understand what it is that is being asserted by theists, and that they know the kinds of things which count for and against theism. Even though belief in the existence of God is held in such a way as to be compatible with any known or knowable state of affairs, and thus is not subject to verification in terms of any appeal to particular experiences, it is legitimate to speak of such a claim as a hypothesis. It is a hypothesis in the same way in which any metaphysical assertion is a hypothesis, even though its adequacy is much more difficult to establish. Its rejection involves an inspection of its claims and a rejection of their adequacy, and it involves the affirmation of the adequacy of an alternative metaphysical description. In short, that it is impossible to prove or disprove theism on the basis of any easily performed test does not affect its status as a hypothesis, for no world hypothesis can be proved or disproved by means of that sort of test.

The Testing of Theistic Assertions

Four types of proofs for theism have been mentioned at various points in the course of this investigation. These are listed and evaluated together here in order to summarize the conclusions of this inquiry as they pertain to the validating of the theistic perspective.

1. It is sometimes claimed that the existence of God can be established conclusively in terms of ordinary verification tech-

niques since there are certain normal experiences and/or crucial experiments which constitute public evidence, and which ought to convince any truly open-minded empiricist. The theological movement known as "empirical theology" has made such claims. In addition, Roman Catholics, and many rather conservative Protestants, claim that there are certain kinds of events which are miraculous and which can be explained only as interventions of God. These events take place on the observable level and violate natural laws in an objectively viewable manner, hence constitute compelling factual evidence. Typically such claims are made in behalf of nature and healing "miracles," fulfillment of prophecy, and claims that the Church is of such nature that its characteristics can only be explained by invoking Divine inspiration. Catholic thinkers will frequently point to the "marks" of the Church, its infallibility, its universality, and so on, as indicators of this sort.[2]

2. It may be claimed that theism is verifiable in terms of *special* or private kinds of experiences, and that only those who have the requisite experiences are able to know God and to understand reality correctly. Self-authenticating revelations, separate radically from ordinary experience, furnish indubitable knowledge of the Divine reality. Revelation, or sometimes mystical experience, is held to be the criterion by which the truth of theistic assertions, or of mystical assertions, is verified, and no appeal beyond this is either possible or legitimate. Such claims are made both by fideists, represented herein by Alasdair MacIntyre, and by mystics such as W. T. Stace, although they are in radical disagreement with each other both as to the kind of Divine reality which is revealed and as to the kind of experience which provides access to God.

It is also often claimed that these experiences are available publically, that is, that they will occur for those who meet the tests, who prepare themselves morally and by rigorous discipline for these experiences. When the experiences do come, it is claimed, they bear their own authenticity with them.

3. At times the assertion is made that theism can be proved in the strictest sense of that word, that certain general features of reality or of rationality require or prove the existence of God. The cosmological form of this argument has already received considerable exposition in earlier discussion.

To the inevitable question as to why there are people who do not accept this proof, the answer is made that those who fail to acknowledge God's existence have blinded themselves to what is really obvious. Sometimes the blame is laid on materialistic modes of explanation or on materialistic concerns, sometimes on prejudice, on sophistication, or on lack of perceptivity. Adherents of this position often go on to claim that true vision will lead to an acknowledgment of God's existence.

The arguments are of two major types: those which root the proofs in an awareness of contingency or of order, and those which root them in some logical awareness. In the latter case it is argued at times that the very notion of truth requires God's existence, or that rationality requires it; or sometimes the familiar ontological argument is employed.

4. Theism is verified, it is sometimes claimed, in terms of its superior adequacy as a metaphysical description. Argument for the truth of theism depends upon the same basic appeals as are made in behalf of any metaphysical description. Those who urge this approach would attempt to develop theism in terms of its metaphysical implications, pointing to those facts and/or aspects of experience which are illuminated by theistic interpretation, and arguing for the acceptance of theism on the basis of such claims. Typical examples are appeals to theistic analyses of the self, of historical development, of evolutionary process,

of rational and moral order, of religious needs in man, and so on. Attention might be directed to the nature of man's sins or shortcomings, his desires for rationality and his striving for moral order, and his refusal to abandon the quest for transcendence, as evidence of his participation in a religious relation of some kind. Effort would be made to persuade the dubious to adopt the theistic perspective in order to gain the view on things which will enable them to validate theistic claims.

This appeal is understood to be noncoercive because it is recognized that other perspectives also yield metaphysical views which seem adequate to their adherents. And yet the perspective is confessed because it seems true, it seems to provide an angle of vision which illuminates reality more adequately than any other.

There are four parallel approaches to the disestablishing of theism. There are those who hold that crucial cases cannot or do not establish the truth of theism, that miracles cannot exist, that all experiments fail, or that the existence of God cannot legitimately be inferred from this kind of experiment. Secondly, there are those who rule out, either in principle or because they do not share them, all special experiences, and who interpret all claims to speak from "privileged" positions as resulting from misinterpretation of ordinary experience. Thirdly, there are those who reject all appeals to so-called universal characteristics, adding, sometimes, that even if valid the arguments could not establish the kind of God that they are used to establish. Moreover, there have been those who have advanced arguments to prove the impossibility of God, that is, that the concept of God is self-contradictory or that such a God could not possibly exist. Lastly, there are those who argue not only that theism is inadequate but that some particular nontheistic metaphysics is more adequate.

It remains only to recapitulate some of the arguments for the fourth approach and to attempt to show, in addition, that the first three approaches either must be reduced to the fourth or must be rejected because they fail to accomplish what they claim to accomplish, or because they are inadequate as descriptions of what actually takes place in discussion of theism.

In the case of the first approach, if appeal is made to the kind of evidence which *can* be agreed upon relatively independently of metaphysical perspective, then the evidence is not conclusive. If the appeal is to any other kind of evidence, then the fourth approach is really being used. For example, if an appeal is made to "death" or to "evil" in the biological and psychological senses, then neither theism nor nontheism is established or disestablished. If, however, appeal is made to death and evil as ultimate and irrational absurdities, then appeal is being made to a particular view of the meaning of evil and death, a nontheistic view, a view which is being offered as the most adequate perspective on death, more adequate than the usual theistic position. The argument, then, is between two competing metaphysical perspectives, to be arbitrated by the test of adequacy.

It has been argued that the second approach is not supported by the way in which theistic discussion actually takes place. It would be possible in theory to base metaphysics purely upon *sui generis* experiences, but theists have not as a rule done this. Theists have appealed to other kinds of experience to illuminate their claims, have responded to changes in science and psychology by altering the meaning of their claims about God and the world, and have argued with their opponents just as though they thought that they and their opponents were talking meaningfully to each other about the same things. The theory that theistic assertions *are* affected by an examination of the whole of experience, that claims to "authority" are evaluated, criticized, modified, and provided with metaphysical backgrounds and justifications, is the fourth type of approach.

Even supposing that the claim be granted that all those who prepare for religious experience will have it, there is still the possibility that they will not interpret it religiously. There are individuals who report experiences which seem to be at least similar to religious experiences but who do not interpret these as indicating anything above or beyond human consciousness. And even supposing that all of them did interpret these experiences religiously, which they do not, the case would not be proved. One may feel quite certain about one's interpretation of an experience and be quite wrong, as is evidenced by strong feelings of certainty connected with delusional states. Moreover, universality of interpretation *could* be due to the way in which one is taught to interpret experiences of that sort.

The third approach, that there is a "perennial philosophy" derived from universal or indubitable characteristics of reality or of logic, can also be taken in two ways. It can be taken as simply one hypothesis, one world view, to be tested, that is, as a case of the fourth approach, or it can be taken as a claim that there actually is, and can be proved to be, a single true metaphysical system. Disagreement among theistic metaphysicians, the existence of conflicting "perennial philosophies" and actual modifications which have taken place in the metaphysical descriptions themselves, the inability of these philosophers to convince nonadherents of their "errors," and the obvious circularity, whether vicious or not, of their method of argument (that is, the premise "the world is contingent" contains within itself the conclusion that "there is a Necessary Being") all can be taken to indicate difficulties in maintaining the claim that there is a "perennial philosophy" in this sense.

The fourth approach involves treating theism as a legitimate metaphysical hypothesis, to be tested as all metaphysical hypotheses are tested, with due consideration given to the type of hypothesis that it claims to be and to the methods and types of beings which are appropriate to its claims. Any metaphysical hypothesis is, in principle, admissable. The fourth approach does not involve dictating to any metaphysical system the type of rules of evidence, criteria of truth, or kinds and levels of description which must be employed. Revelations, whether they be of mystical, dialogical, propositional, scientific, or any other kind, may and must be tested in terms of the adequacy of the insights which they produce.

The attempt in earlier chapters has been to indicate the impossibility of simple solutions to metaphysical questions, whether it be "crucial cases" or particular epistemological methods or particular doctrines for the interpretation of symbols or particular perennial philosophies to which appeal has been made. The circularity of all metaphysical appeals has been indicated, but a circularity which is open to modification because the reference of metaphysical systems is to the world. It has been shown that metaphysics must be circular, confessional in character, an attempt to understand the nature of things which is subject to biases and predecisions and to the finiteness of every perceiver.

It should also be pointed out that there is no possible basis for disproving theism in any conclusive way. Bertrand Russell was earlier cited as observing that he knows of no way of disproving God's existence, and the kinds of difficulties examined in the earlier discussion of naturalism indicated that the alleged objections were inconclusive. The conclusive proof or disproof of religious or other metaphysical views is not possible.

Metaphysical views are total views, and thus they have provided some means of accounting for every kind of evidence known or they would not be adequate world views. Holders of each view believe that they have accounted, at least in principle, for all the kinds of facts of which they know, and that any puzzles still unsolved are capable of solution, at least theoretically, in terms of the categories of their system. In both the examples which follow this very point is made.

Naturalists know that they are unable at present to predict exactly what the future will be, hence that they cannot "cash in" determinism or even such basic principles as the uniformity of nature. However, this is not particularly embarrassing to the naturalist, for he is sure that when future events happen they will be in principle predictable and uniform with the rest of nature. The naturalist realizes that, as a matter of fact, he cannot cover all the cases, even in the present; however, he also "knows" that nothing will happen which will contradict his naturalistic explanations.

Likewise, the theologian believes that difficult cases, such as cases of apparently absolute evil, are resolvable in terms of theistic categories even when he cannot see exactly how to resolve the problems. He can supply reasons why he is not in a position to resolve the problems, such as that he cannot see good and evil from God's point of view or that he cannot measure the long-run consequences of particular present events. Since he believes that God is good and powerful, he "knows" that no absolute evil ever happens, therefore that cases of apparent absolute evil can be resolved, but not by him.

John Hick's comment on theism, that there seems to be no amount of evidence "in face of which it would be demonstrably irrational to maintain theistic belief," [3] has already been noted but is worthy of repetition. The comment applies equally well to other positions, for no amount of logical and/or factual argument could bring the mystic to the point at which it would be demonstrably irrational to maintain mystical belief, no naturalist could be brought to deny naturalistic belief, and so on.

It is sometimes thought that the rise of science and scientific modes of explanation has forced theism from the metaphysical scene, or at least has caused drastic modification in theistic ideas. The truth of the matter, however, is that, although some ideas of theists about matters of science have changed, the constitutive categories of theistic metaphysics are little altered. W. T. Stace, a keen critic of theism and defender of naturalistic views of the space-time world, points out that although there has been a marked decline in theistic theories in the modern world, a decline which began with the rise of modern science, the rise of modern science has had no *logical* effect on theism one way or the other. His claim is "that no scientific argument . . . can ever have the slightest tendency either to prove or to disprove the existence of God; in short that science is irrelevant to religion." [4] It makes no difference either to theism or to atheism whether the sun goes around the earth or the earth goes around the sun, or whether they both go around something else.

Stace goes on to claim, however, that the case for theism has been weakened psychologically, particularly by the substitution of mechanical causes for teleological causes in modern science, and by the fact that in the Copernican and post-Copernican worlds man is no longer physically the center of a small universe which seems to have been built around him. Thus it is no longer so easy for man to think of his world theistically. However, since psychological ease is not a criterion of truth but only of psychological ease, the logical case for theism has not been affected, and is, factually and logically speaking, no better and no worse than it ever was, as far as its basic claims are concerned.

The same remarks apply when one considers the proof of theism. The situation is really unaltered with respect to proof.

Whereas theistic perspectives were psychologically easier in an age when theistic interpretation ruled the minds of men, when anxieties about finitude were answered theologically, and when questions about ultimate origin were asked and answered theistically, their logical case was actually exactly the same as it is now. Men did not then know that there were alternative metaphysical interpretations which could "do justice to" the whole of human experience, and they were not even psychologically ready to entertain such ideas, perhaps. However, this obviously has nothing to do with the logical status of those beliefs. That a belief is universal is not a proof of its truth, as is acknowledged by the recognition on the part of many philosophers that no strict proof of the existence of even the external world is possible, although everyone believes in that world.

The point being made is simply that the case for theism, from the logical or metaphysical point of view, is unaltered by recent developments in science and by recent awareness of cultural and other relativisms. The psychological case has been altered, for theism is no longer psychologically obvious, but the logical case has not changed, and this means that theism's case never was stronger logically than it now is. It is not that theism's logical power has been reduced, but that its base in faith has now been exposed, a development welcomed by some able theologians.

In the chapter which follows an attempt will be made to summarize the basic contentions in this book concerning metaphysical method and its relations to factuality, symbol systems, and logical methods, conclusions which will reinforce those just reached in this chapter. The test for metaphysical truth is adequacy, and adequacy is a function of perspective, and perspective is a function of what ought to be called "faith."

VIII. Metaphysics and Proof

Of central concern throughout this book has been the question of the nature of metaphysical thinking. Metaphysics, the concern for a general theory of reality, has been presented in terms of a perspectivist or root-metaphor theory of truth. It has been argued that metaphysical thinking is most adequately described as perspectival, that metaphysical theories are built up out of root metaphors which themselves depend upon judgments as to what things or ideas are ultimately of significance. This claim has been defended in terms of an analysis of philosophical disagreement, an analysis of basic issues in a sample metaphysical dispute, an analysis of theological statements, an analysis of the nature of metaphysical thinking itself, and an analysis of symbols and interpretation rules.

This particular theory of metaphysics has been presented both as a description of the way in which many philosophers actually proceed and themselves understand metaphysical thinking, and as the only valid way to understand the processes of metaphysical thought considering the facts brought to light in the various analyses of which this study is comprised. Thus the study consists of both supporting quotations from philosophical writings and analyses of the problems which led philosophers to make such assertions.

It has been indicated from time to time that there are other theories of the nature of metaphysics which differ from this perspectivist theory. Two types of competing theory have been discussed, both theories holding that there is a single metaphysical position, the truth of which can be conclusively demonstrated in some way. Some final comments on these two alternative theories seem to be in order.

1. Sometimes the claim is made that there is a "perennial philosophy," a metaphysical description which is acknowledged, dimly or openly, by all men who think correctly and see rightly, a single position which is the logical culmination of sound reasoning, to which all opponents can be driven by logic or by factual demonstration. This claim has been made by positivists, of whose views Lazerowitz provides a good example, by classicists and Neo-Thomists, by some naturalists, and by mystics, to take only the examples utilized in this study.

The fact that there are so many candidates for the throne of "perennial philosophy" and the fact that each claimant is rejected by all other pretenders who put forth their own positions as objectively provable makes it difficult to hold to the theory. The theory cannot be proved false; however, doubt as to its validity can be raised. The mere presence of multiple candidates would itself seem to indicate the need for some way to test the claims of the various alternatives. If the proof of the pudding is in the eating, if the proof of the claim that there is a single position which ought to be acknowledged by all reasonable men is whether or not all apparently reasonable men agree, then the claim is not borne out by the philosophical facts. Philosophers continue to disagree despite all the logical and factual arguments and counterarguments brought to bear in behalf of particular views.

Moreover, the indications that there may be subjectivizing factors in the very processes of thinking and seeing would themselves indicate grounds for skepticism even were there no competing claimants. Particular metaphysical views may be true, but because adequacy is a function of perspective, one has no right to assume that the view is true merely because it seems to be. Once the possibility of relativizing factors in metaphysical method has been brought into the open, then it would seem to be clear that one has to check to see whether one's views have caused him to be misled. The mere possibility of subjectivism makes certainty dubious, until its claims have been tested. If this is admitted, then certainty has been abandoned as the test for metaphysical views, and this view reduces to another metaphysical method.

2. The second alternative metaphysical method is the method of absolute authority. Advocates of this theory of metaphysics might agree that philosophical disputes cannot be settled in terms of appeals to ordinary facts and logical rules, yet insist that truth can be established on other grounds, in terms of an appeal to some authority or authoritative type of experience.

This statement has to be clarified to prevent confusion. One might want to hold that truth is revealed by some authority, or tested in terms of some authoritative experience, and yet maintain that claims which arise in this manner need to be tested. There are many irreconcilable metaphysical propositions which have been asserted on the basis of authority, and it might be that one would want to put these claims to some test, perhaps by testing whether or not the views they yield are adequate as descriptions of the nature of things. Thus one might say that knowledge about reality is given by God, and yet insist that claims made in behalf of particular propositions allegedly derived from God be tested. God might be the authority for metaphysical truth, yet some of the propositions attributed by men to God be mistaken. Since various and incompatible interpretations of God's revealed truth have been offered by different religious groups, it would seem that some must be in error and that metaphysical testing might be in order.

However, it might be that no test of authority is possible, that the authority must be accepted on its own testimony or not at all. Those who hold to the method of absolute authority as opposed to the method of tentative acceptance of authority described above would claim that truth is given by God and in no other way, and that it must be accepted without question since there is no other criterion in terms of which it can be judged.

Such a theory would be perfectly compatible with the present state of metaphysical diversity, for the theory does not require that all men agree. Rather it states that only those who accept the required authority will know truth, and that advocates of all positions based on something else will know falsely. What is an embarrassment, however, is the presence of competing propositions allegedly derived from the same authority. Then, to maintain the position, one must hold that there is no independent criterion which enables one to distinguish the propositions which really come from the authority and those which do not since their authoritativeness is the only legitimate test. If one admits that there are other kinds of tests, then one has abandoned absolute authority. However, what then is done about the presence of several groups, each claiming loyalty to the authority, each claiming authoritativeness for its own versions of the pronouncements of that authority? If one tests in terms of some independent criterion, then the method is lost; if one cannot, then there is no way to adjudicate among the competing claims, for each is put forward as authoritative.

It is logically possible that this position be true, for the mere fact that a number of competing theories are put forward on the same basis does not indicate necessarily that they are all false or all true. It might be that one claimant speaks truly and all others speak falsely, and that there is no reason, factual or logical, on the basis of which it could be decided which is which. There is no way to prove this theory false; however, it is possible to show that it is not adhered to in practice.

While adherence to this method is logically possible, it has been argued that in practice many of those who claim to follow this method actually seem to do something else. It has been argued that many of those who claim to adhere to authoritarian systems actually do change their views with the philosophical times. The point was made, for example, that even the kind of appeal made by Alasdair MacIntyre is basically of the twentieth century, although, of course, it has occurred from time to time before this, and that it is quite different from the classical Christian view of which it claims to be a continuation. It has been argued that neither in the early period nor in its later history has the Church followed the method of absolute authority; rather it has offered factual and logical grounds for believing in God.

Moreover, as has already been noted, theological doctrines have, in the past, been stated in philosophical language, not by means of a private vocabulary. As philosophical language changes or as different languages are used to express theological insights the content of religion seems to change. Thus some commentators have alleged that the mere translation of biblical religion into Greek effected some rather radical changes in the content of theology, and it is rather obvious, at least to many, that the ideas of various theologians and the interpretations that they put on Scriptures and tradition reflect the times of the theologian as well as those of the tradition.

However, all this fails to constitute a refutation of absolute authority as a method. At best, these comments merely indicate that many of those who have claimed to follow the method have done something else instead, and it is quite possible to argue that any concessions which have been made to philosophical change have been in error or that the appearance of change is deceiving, that theology should have developed a language of its own with its own private meanings accessible only to believers or that theology has in fact developed such a private language, all appearances to the contrary notwithstanding.

In short, the position is a possible one, but it does not seem to be the case that it is actually followed. Theologians may think that they are following such a method but their actual conclusions are relative to their own times. Many adherents to the method of absolute authority actually utilize the method of tentative authority; that is, they question doctrines, change formulations, adopt new ideas, as a reflection of scientific, philosophical, and general cultural change.

Whether or not the foregoing observations establish the conclusion that the method of tentative hypothesis is the *only* legitimate method in metaphysics, it has been made clear in Chapter Four that there is at least a very wide agreement that this is the method which ought to be used. Previous discussion has indicated that a number of philosophers, advocates of widely divergent metaphysical theories, agree that the only legitimate methodology is that defended here.

The Testing of Metaphysical Assertions

It has been argued that metaphysical assertions cannot be disproved on purely logical and objective grounds because metaphysical assertions are or can be made to seem to be compatible with any conceivable state of affairs. Nevertheless, metaphysical descriptions are sometimes abandoned as their adequacy is questioned. At least the following five types of question have to be considered in establishing or disestablishing the adequacy of a metaphysical description.

1. Since a metaphysical description is developed from a particular field or a particular selection of data which is thought to be of significance, the adequacy of a metaphysical description must be evaluated in terms of the exactness of its "fit" in that field. New knowledge, and the creation of new perspectives and hypotheses within the field, the continued stubbornness of particular problems within the field, and insights or categories arising from other fields of knowledge may suggest changes in basic descriptions. Openness to alternative systems of categories may accomplish the same end.

2. Since the creation of metaphysical hypotheses involves the extension of descriptions into fields other than the one in which the hypotheses arose, questions of "fit" there must also be raised. The set of hypotheses must be applicable to every field, either in terms of directly providing the categories useful in interpreting the data and lesser schema of abstraction in each field or in terms of providing categories under which the lesser schema can be subsumed. Difficulties sometimes indicate weakness in the generating metaphor, but sometimes merely weakness in ingenuity in applying this metaphor to the new field; hence their presence need not overthrow the hypotheses. However, full adequacy cannot be reached until such difficulties are solved, at least in principle.

3. There are also certain questions which must be asked of a metaphysical description as a whole—the theory must be free from logical errors and inconsistencies, and the conclusions which follow from the description and the presuppositions and assumptions which underlie the description should be drawn out, challenged, and defended or rejected. The exposing and challenging of assumptions may alter significantly a major part of a meta-

physical description, or actually lead to its overthrow. Under the impact of such questioning, many "self-evident" ideas have lost their self-evidence. Such seems to have happened to the cosmological, ontological, and teleological arguments, to the idea of simple location so basic to many atomisms, to the "verification principle" and the appeal to "plain facts," whether "miracles" or sense data or religious experiences, at least for a large part of the modern intellectual world.[1]

4. Since metaphysical descriptions are *world* views, and since it has been shown that the relevance of evidence is dictated, in part, by theory, very important in the testing of a metaphysical hypothesis should be the entertaining of alternative hypotheses. This has importance for a number of reasons, as a check against undue subjectivism in one's own description, as a means of discovering possible alternatives which are more adequate than one's own description, and as a means of illuminating hitherto unnoticed or underemphasized aspects of the nature of things.

Since competing metaphysical systems present different views on reality, the attempt to entertain these views might be of great help in overcoming the deficiencies of one's own. Not that one is ever able really to see things wholly as others see them—to do so would be to enter another perspective—but one can more or less see what others are talking about. The entertaining of other alternatives may very well help one to see the possible narrowness of his own.

5. The reasons why one particular description and no other seems to be most adequate should be investigated carefully, for it is here that metaphysical discussion may be most fruitful. Theists have argued, for example, that a theistic hypothesis points to and accounts for certain aspects of the nature of things which cannot be satisfactorily accounted for in nontheistic terms. Other descriptions, for example, fail to "do justice" to certain

features of the world, such as its order, or the alleged gradual triumph of good, or man's hunger for the infinite, or the self-transcendence of man, or miracles, or perhaps the purity of the saints. In fact, if there *is* to be any argument for the superiority of any metaphysical description it perhaps must be of this type— a pointing to aspects of experience or to some particular experiences which are adequately explained, allegedly, only on the basis of this particular theory. Since the justification for holding a metaphysical theory is the illumination which it brings to all subject matters, attention must be paid to what the particular theory illuminates that other theories do not deal with as well.

There is no guarantee that attention to any of these tests will change metaphysical views in basic respects. In fact, it is doubtful that it will, and yet there are no other tests than these. Philosophers have disagreed and will disagree, a fact about which some lament but others rejoice.

Difficulties in Testing

Metaphysical disputes are factual, not logical, but they are not the kind of disputes which can be settled in terms of appeals to plain fact, because different metaphysical positions offer different theories as to what the facts really are. Different theories present different perspectives in which to view the plain facts.

Logical rules, rules for symbol interpretation, and appeals to observation are all relative to metaphysical views, and their validity is established by the adequacy of the metaphysical views which generate them. Logical atomism is legitimized by metaphysical atomism, mystical experience by metaphysical mysticism, the way of analogy by the great-chain-of-being kind of metaphysical view. One cannot begin with self-evident logical rules, views of facts, sentence structures, or symbol rules. Rather, one must hold all such views provisionally. Validation comes at the end, not at the beginning, of the metaphysical quest, and even at the end there is no logical certainty.

The fact that a consistent theory can be worked out does not itself establish the truth of the system. This is the case not only because there are a number of theories which seem consistent to their advocates but also because the final criterion for metaphysical truth is adequacy, not consistency. Adequacy is the final criterion because the goal of metaphysical thinking is a description of the facts.

It is perhaps true that ultimately a metaphysical system must be consistent, but it is obviously the case that not every consistent system is true. It could not be, for there are many competing, seemingly consistent, systems, and since they conflict with one another, not all of them can be true. Besides, there is nothing to prevent a system's being consistently false, particularly since it is clear that facts can be "made" to fit systems. As Gordon Kaufman has pointed out, increasing consistency of conceptual schema and success in interpreting reality by using its categories may mean merely that "we are gradually working out, with increasing success, a coherent pattern of what is ultimately a false view of reality," and he adds the alarming observation that, in such a case, "we come to believe increasingly that the presuppositions on which we are operating are true when they may in fact be false, and the more we 'verify' them, the less able we are to believe in their possible falsity." [2] Thus the very consistency with which the false position can be elaborated helps to protect it from a detection of its underlying false presuppositions.

It is the adequacy of the perspective which it articulates, the usefulness of the logical rules it employs, the "fit" of the symbol system which it generates, that is the test for the truth of metaphysical systems. However, it is obvious that, even though adequacy is the final test, it does not enable one to decide for certain among systems. The fact is that there are many metaphysical views, each of which must seem to be adequate to its adherents or else they would not hold it. Thus, although adequacy *is* the final test, the test yields different results to different people.

Systems change, but largely in terms of refinements which are internal to the system, in terms of changing a concept here, a rule there, within the framework of the system as a whole. Thus theists may now assert that the creation took place a much longer time ago than they used to think, and naturalists may now admit that the religious dimension of life is of greater importance to the psyche than they used to think, but no new facts or rules will be advanced that can overthrow the larger metaphysical frameworks. As has already been argued with respect to the theism-naturalism controversy, one cannot imagine a new factual situation which would be decisive since each position would fit the new situation into its own structure.

The positions are too well established by their success, by their entrenchment in the very rules which seem to be logical and the very facts which seem to be evidential, to be overthrown. Moreover, the positions are too well reinforced against competing theories to be overthrown. Persons may change systems, but they cannot be compelled to by factual or logical argument. What is being pointed out here is a matter not merely of psychology but of metaphysics.

The claim made in the initial chapter that philosophical positions are based on something akin to what religions have called faith thus seems true beyond question. A philosophical position is based upon a particular view of reality which cannot itself be justified except in terms of the adequacy of the system to which it gives rise, and which itself helps supply the view of the world used to test its own adequacy.

This is not to say that philosophical views are based wholly upon faiths, but merely that they reflect the faiths on the basis of which man structures his view of the world. There is a world of some sort to which man is related, and metaphysical theories arise out of man's effort to understand that world; yet man does not see that world, think about that world, or know that world apart from the presuppositions which affect his view of it.

To articulate one's metaphysical views is thus to confess one's faith, and it is also to work out the consequences of that faith that it might be tested. Such a claim does not constitute pure subjectivism because one is confessing a view on the world, a view which has been formed by looking on that world in an effort to see it steadily and whole, but which has also been formed in terms of the fundamental experiences, logical judgments, and perspectives which constitute one's view. Moreover, one confesses his views usually in concert with others whose views of reality are similarly shaped, and in dialogue with different perspectives presented by those of other philosophical faiths, both of which help to check against pure subjectivity; but one cannot be sure of one's group, one's adversaries, or one's rejection or acceptance of their positions. Checking of views against compatible and incompatible claims helps to guard against subjectivism, but it does not provide a guarantee.

An additional check is made possible by the fact that many of the problems that one works with are relatively standard problems, and by the fact that there are a number of more or less well-defined sets of abstractions and tested theories, the various sciences both natural and social, religions, ethical systems and values, all of which are relatively well-established sets of abstractions, which must in some sense be taken into account. Here is another extra-systematic factor in metaphysical thinking. Yet, though the problems are standard, though the systems of abstraction are more or less acknowledged in common, the answers to these problems, decisions as to how the various sets of abstractions are to be interpreted and related to one another, what one does with these more limited claimants to knowledge, all these differ markedly from philosopher to philosopher.

One does find conversions, radical shifts in perspective, but not often. The changes in views usually found are relatively minor and constitute mere internal modifications within systems. Elements within a metaphysical view may be modified rather painlessly at times. It seems also to be true that one may adopt to a degree different perspectives temporarily, trying them on for size, so to speak. Moreover, major or minor elements within a metaphysical position may be doubted, at least tentatively, without radical metaphysical shifts taking place. However, one cannot cast aside whole perspectives without radical change. Since one's metaphysical perspective forms his whole frame of mind and perception, it cannot be discarded without a radical restructuring of the self. The mystic seems to be right in his recognition that metaphysical conversion involves destruction of the whole sensory-intellectual habits of the self and the rebuilding of a new self, a phenomenon often evidenced by former "believers" of all sorts.

It has been argued that metaphysical descriptions are confessional. This is not to argue that metaphysical descriptions are deliberately subjective, for such is not the case. A metaphysical description represents an effort at objectivity, at finding the most adequate description, at specifying what must be said in order to interpret the nature of things. Each description represents a careful and detailed effort to coordinate the whole of human knowledge, to account for all aspects of existence. The process of developing and testing a metaphysical description demands utmost care, constant appraisal and reappraisal of theories and descriptive terms, efforts to resolve puzzles and to simplify apparatus; in short, the most careful thinking that can be done. It is not a matter of setting out to see things in whatever way one wants to see them, but rather an effort to see things the way that they are. Nevertheless, serious and careful thinkers do disagree in their metaphysical descriptions, and not all differences can be reconciled.

The chief disadvantage of this general theory of metaphysics is that it seems to be compatible with every form of fantastic speculation that can be developed into a total description. There is no limit to the kinds of ghosts and dimensions of reality which have been proposed as metaphysical theories and no limit to the special avenues to truth which can be claimed. Systems of magic, astrology, gnosticism, animism, and "gremlinism" are perhaps subject to elaboration and defense, despite the fact that the intellectual world as a whole has repudiated them as inadequate. The fact is, however, that there is no purely logical reason for repudiating them, that there is no clear and unprejudicial criterion by which they must be rejected, that there is no possible disproof of their claims except in terms of an appeal to what seems to be a "more adequate" explanation, that is, except in terms of an appeal to a different perspective or set of concepts which is held to be more adequate.

There seems to be no escape, at least no sure escape, from the point Ben Kimpel is making in the following statement:

Hypotheses differ in their credibility for an individual because each individual assumes certain points of view, and these points of view he employs as criteria with which he evaluates other points of view. The particular point of view with which an interpretation of a reality is evaluated is an assumption about that reality. Hence, one hypothesis about a reality is evaluated only when another hypothesis is assumed as probably more informed of the nature of that reality. The rejection of an hypothesis, therefore, may reveal more about the confidence which an individual has in what he regards as knowledge than it discloses about the actual untenability of an hypothesis.[3]

Neither consistency nor adequacy offers a sure avenue of escape because neither ensures that subjectivity is eliminated.

Metaphysics and Proof

It has been argued that proof in the strictest sense is impossible, that metaphysical descriptions are functions of particular perspectives which must be shared in order for the perspective to be seen to be adequate. Attention has been called to the difficulty of comparing descriptions with reality, both because descriptions are human descriptions, the products of human experience and symbolizing, and because interpretations of reality are already metaphysized. Criteria for the facts, legitimate methods of investigation, proper limits for speculation, and competence of witnesses are all related to particular metaphysical descriptions and cannot be specified in independence of particular points of view.

Metaphysics is an attempt to bring divergent intuitions into harmony with the nature of things, but it is also a critique of cosmologies. Metaphysical descriptions are tested, in part, in terms of their adequacy in accounting for more specialized descriptions, yet they also serve as a basis for the criticism of descriptions of more specialized aspects of things from the standpoint of a total theory. Specialized descriptions are themselves in process of formulation and thus do not form a secure base for erecting metaphysical descriptions. On the other hand, a metaphysical description is not so certain that it can be used as an infallible guide for the criticism of specialized descriptions.

The categories and basic methods of particular specialized bodies of knowledge or, rather, of the various candidates for the status of knowledge in more specialized areas of human inquiry

cannot simply be accepted without question, for their adequacy
is tested in part by their being fitted into a metaphysical description. The validity of a particular specialized perspective, its
relative importance with reference to other perspectives, the
adequacy of the metaphysical implications of its categories and
methods, all these are measured in part in terms of a total theory
of reality as well as in terms of the specialized field itself.

Because of this dialectical interplay there are always two opposite dangers in metaphysics. One danger is that some authentic
area of human knowledge or some authentic perspective upon
the nature of things has been excluded by the premature adoption of a too-narrow metaphysical description. Simplification is
essential, but every simplification may be an oversimplification.
The opposite danger is that some body of specialized "knowledge" may have been assumed to constitute knowledge when it
is largely false or seriously misleading. For example, a metaphysical description which excludes the facts of theism might thereby
be inadequate. On the other hand, the "facts" of theism may
not be facts at all and to include them as basic facts in metaphysics would then be to distort. In the first case, there is premature exclusion of valid data; in the second case, there is
premature inclusion of the invalid as data. To combat the first
danger, there is need for continued scrutiny of excluded possibilities; to combat the second danger, there is need for continued
reexamination of what has been retained within the system.

There are more *possible* metaphysical theories than there seem
to be *live* metaphysical positions. If one appeals to those positions
which have been able to win a considerable number of adherents,
the possibilities are narrowed considerably. Number of adherents,
of course, is not a test for truth, yet it would seem, and seem
is a perspective word, feasible to restrict one's attention to those
positions to which rather sizable numbers of critical philosophers

adhere. If one does this, then metaphysical positions can be reduced to a limited number of root metaphors, or can be grouped according to a limited number of fields of origination. In the modern Western world, there seem to be three basic groupings of metaphysical theories, those arising out of appeals to reason, those arising out of appeals to revelation, and those arising out of appeals to experience. There have been, of course, many differing theories within each tradition and many combinations and overlappings of theories; nevertheless, the threefold classification holds in general. A metaphysical description in order to be adequate must provide fruitful hypotheses for the interpretation of the results of all three of these traditions. Not that dominant theories in each must be retained, but that effort must be made to deal with the continuing presence of these three traditions. Inability to achieve some degree of adequacy in all three is a serious defect in metaphysics.

For the modern thinker, it seems to be the case that a metaphysical hypothesis, whatever else it may be compatible with, must be compatible with scientific knowledge. Whether the reason that this has been so is that the modern world is biased toward science, which is possible, or whether it is because scientific knowledge has been established in such a way that, although scientific knowledge does change and although there may be ever so many other aspects of reality to take into account, the present results of scientific investigation will never be totally repudiated, it has been true that metaphysical descriptions in the modern world attempt to "do justice to" (a perspective phrase) scientific knowledge. This is increasingly true even of mystical traditions.

There is uncertainty in science, but this uncertainty has to do with the precision of scientific descriptions and with the question as to the *extent* of the validity of scientific method. That science is dealing with real things and that it has validity as one road to truth seems to be taken as certain by nearly all modern Western thinkers. The uncertainty with regard to the things with which classical philosophy and religion have been concerned is of another kind, for there are quite genuine and widespread doubts as to whether the concepts which these two traditions have used have objective referents. That people do think in terms of classical philosophical and religious concepts is true, descriptively. That they still have any right to think in these terms is in question. To have pointed out that this right is in question is not to have pointed to any answer to the question. It may have been to point only to something which has always been known, that the question of God is not like the question of rocks and trees, and that to "see" God requires a response rather different from seeing a sunset.

Nevertheless, no metaphysical description can be considered to be adequate unless some account is given of the areas with which traditional philosophy and religion have been concerned. That man can create gods is an important datum for science. That man perhaps *responds* to God is more important yet.

To have analyzed the basic problems of metaphysics, to have shown what can and what cannot be done in metaphysics, to have raised and to have disposed of some of the major modern objections to metaphysics, to have mentioned and to have cast doubt upon some of the basic appeals which have been used both in metaphysics and in theology, to have indicated the convergence of a number of factors in modern and recent thought upon a conception of metaphysics and religion which has made renewed philosophical discussion both possible and necessary, is not to have created an adequate metaphysical description. The creation of a metaphysical description is a separate task. To become aware of points of possible arbitrariness ought to be a step in the direction of less dogmatism, and to have a summary and exposition of some of the points of possible arbitrariness in metaphysics and theology ought to be a step in the direction of such an awareness.

That metaphysics is inescapable, but that every metaphysic is, or at least cannot be known infallibly not to be, relative to some basic perspective, and that there are no infallible appeals which avoid this relativity in any complete way, has been the conclusion of this inquiry. That metaphysics is nonetheless open-ended to a degree, that metaphysical descriptions are functions of the nature of things as well as of perspectives upon these things, and therefore that it is possible to alter metaphysical descriptions in the direction of greater adequacy to the nature of things has also been concluded, both from actual developments which have taken place in metaphysics and from consideration of the nature of metaphysics itself. This awareness explains both why philosophers disagree and why it is important to go on disagreeing, for out of the sharing of insights in disagreement comes reexamination of positions, without which philosophical progress is unlikely.

Notes

1. The solipsist, for example, admits that there *seems* to be a world external to himself, peopled with beings independent of himself. The mystic admits that the appearances of a spatio-temporal world are among us even though they mislead us if we take them to indicate a *real* external world. Likewise, a behaviorist in psychology may admit that there seems to be a mind distinct from the brain but deny that there *really* is.

A story is told of three umpires who disagreed as to what they were doing behind home plate. One claimed that he merely called them as he saw them. The second claimed that he "calls them as they are," but the third maintained that "they ain't nothin' 'til I calls 'em." The "plain facts" are that they call balls and strikes; the critical accounts, the views as to the real facts, differ quite markedly.

2. Laird, *Recent Philosophy*, pp. 250–51.

3. Carnap, *Philosophy and Logical Syntax*, pp. 29–30.

4. Lazerowitz, *The Structure of Metaphysics*, p. 96. Hereafter abbreviated as SM. All of the citations which follow are from this book unless otherwise indicated.

5. Lazerowitz, "The Relevance of Psychoanalysis to Philosophy," in Hook, ed., *Psychoanalysis, Scientific Method, and Philosophy*, pp. 133–56. Hereafter abbreviated as PSP.

6. Ostow and Scharfstein, *The Need to Believe*, p. 146.

One wonders, only half puckishly, what psychoanalytic understanding of Lazerowitz's reasons for offering such a theory of metaphysics could be offered. Why is it that there are philosophers who, although confronted by the "plain facts" of complexity in philosophical matters, refuse to give up their simple-minded (as opposed to complex-minded) solutions to philosophical problems? "And sometimes I think even thee a little queer," the saying goes.

7. Pepper, "The Root Metaphor Theory of Metaphysics," *Journal of Philosophy*, XXXII (July 4, 1935), 365–74. An expanded version of this claim has been published as *World Hypotheses*, and the basic theses are also presented in an article entitled "Metaphysical Method," *Philosophical Review*, LII, 252–69. E. A. Burtt challenges Pepper's thesis that pluralism is inescapable, defending instead the possibility of genuine synthesis of categories, in "The Status of 'World Hypotheses,'" *Philosophical Review,* LII, 590–601.

8. Whorf, *Collected Papers on Metalinguistics*, p. 5.

9. Hick, *Faith and Knowledge*, p. 148.

CHAPTER TWO: *Basic Disputes Are Factual*

1. Hook, "Naturalism and Democracy," in Krikorian, ed., *Naturalism and the Human Spirit*, pp. 42–43 and p. 45.

2. *Ibid.*, p. 45.

3. Lamprecht, "Naturalism and Religion," in Krikorian, ed., *Naturalism and the Human Spirit*, p. 20.

4. *Ibid.*, pp. 31–32 and p. 34.

5. Nagel, "Naturalism Reconsidered," in Krikorian and Edel, eds., *Contemporary Philosophic Problems*, p. 345.

6. *Ibid.*, p. 346.

7. Feigl, "Empiricism Versus Theology," in Edwards and Pap, eds., *A Modern Introduction to Philosophy*, pp. 535–36.

8. There seems to be no event for which it would be impossible to supply some naturalistic explanation whether the event actually be so caused or not. Today's "miracle" may become tomorrow's science, as is perhaps indicated by current researches into so-called extrasensory phenomena. There are no well-authenticated events that are so strange that a supernatural cause *must* be assigned, as many contemporary theologians would be the first to admit.

9. Feigl, "Empiricism Versus Theology," p. 537.

10. Mascall, *He Who Is*, pp. 83 and 3. Italics added.

11. Mascall, *Existence and Analogy*, pp. 80 and 122.

12. Farrer, *Finite and Infinite*, p. 97, and *The Glass of Vision*, p. 89.

13. Copleston, *Aquinas,* p. 114. This section of the book is reprinted in *A Modern Introduction to Philosophy,* edited by P. Edwards and A. Pap. The above quotation can be found on p. 478 of that anthology, which also contains a perceptive discussion of logical positivism by Copleston and A. J. Ayer.

14. Hook, "Modern Knowledge and the Idea of God," *Commentary,* XXIX (1960), 206.

15. There are some who would reject this claim on the ground that the ontological argument successfully derives God's existence from His essence. Since neither Hook nor the Neo-Thomists under consideration advance this claim, and since it is not, in this author's estimation, a valid argument, this claim is being omitted.

16. Russell, *Why I Am Not a Christian,* p. 50.

17. Hook, "Modern Knowledge and the Idea of God," p. 208.

18. It is not legitimate to confine empirically meaningful notions to what men can experience with present instruments right now. The other side of the moon was an empirically meaningful concept prior to space probes. John Hutchison, *Faith, Reason and Existence,* p. 41, makes the same error when he criticizes A. J. Ayer's use of the phrase "a being whose intellect was infinitely powerful" as violating the conditions of empirical meaning. This phrase is empirically meaningful since such a being is logically possible and may be constructed some day.

For whatever it is worth, Fredric Brown has a story of two beings who construct a computer with parts covering every body in a solar system. On asking it their first question, "Is there a God?" the machine replied, "Now there is," destroying the two as they reached desperately for the switch to disconnect the brain.

19. Emmett, *The Nature of Metaphysical Thinking,* p. 12.

20. Hick, "God as Necessary Being," *Journal of Philosophy,* LVII (1960), 726.

21. Jolivet, *The God of Reason,* pp. 37–38 and p. 35.

CHAPTER THREE: *Theology Is Metaphysical*

1. Schlick, "Meaning and Verification," *The Philosophical Review,* XLV (July, 1936), 341.

2. Hutchison, *Faith, Reason and Existence*, p. 157. What has been said concerning viability will need to be reiterated in connection with later discussion of the proposal of some thinkers that "inevitability" or felt "appropriateness" be a suitable criterion for religious symbols. Unless it can be shown that what is "inevitable" is *ipso facto* true, the inevitability of symbols perhaps indicates merely something about the structure of the human psyche.

3. Some theists, however, might expect God's presence to be detectable by experimental means. If God is an energy-system and suitable means to detect such energy were devised, then the question of God's existence becomes one which could in principle be answered experimentally. Since, however, the more usual claim is that God is in principle unexperiencable since he has no material being, this qualification has not been introduced into the main body of discussion.

4. Hartshorne, *Reality as Social Process*, p. 129.

5. Barth, *The Doctrine of the Word of God*, Part I, p. 434.

6. Sittler, "The Necessity of Faith," *Christian Scholar*, XXXVIII (September, 1955), 201–4.

7. *Ibid.*, p. 202.

8. *Ibid.*, p. 204.

9. Popkin, "Theological and Religious Skepticism," *Christian Scholar*, XXXIX (June, 1956), 150–58. Popkin's theory is an intriguing one, for he shows that there are no tests by which one can distinguish between the two lines of skeptics. We usually say that Kierkegaard is a believer and Bayle is not, but the truth of this assertion cannot really be shown.

10. Elsewhere I have tried to show that Martin Buber similarly makes metaphysical assertions about God's nature while at the same time denying that he does so. The reason, in my estimation, for the errors of both Sittler and Buber is that they unwarrantably identify all metaphysical views with rationalism. Their proper enemy is rationalism, not metaphysics. For a discussion of Buber's views, see Frank B. Dilley, "Is There 'Knowledge' of God?" *Journal of Religion*, XXXVIII (April, 1958), 116–26. Buber's reply is contained in Sidney and Beatrice Rome, eds., *Philosophical Interrogations* (New York: Holt, Rinehart, and Winston, 1964).

11. Kroner, *How Do We Know God?* p. 33.

12. *Ibid.*, pp. 33 and 48.

13. James Alfred Martin, Jr., *Empirical Philosophies of Religion*, p. 76.

14. MacIntyre, "The Logical Status of Religious Belief," *Metaphysical Beliefs*, p. 181 and p. 201. For simplification, the page numbers from this work will be inserted in the body of the text.

15. Crombie, "Theology and Falsification," in Flew and MacIntyre, eds., *New Essays in Philosophical Theology*, pp. 122–23.

16. Foster, " 'We' in Modern Philosophy," in Mitchell, ed., *Faith and Logic*, p. 200. These remarks were directed to philosophers such as A. J. Ayer, but are applicable to the use to which I have put them.

17. *Ibid.*, p. 201.

18. *Ibid.*, p. 204.

19. Not only has a large segment of Christian theology denied that creation took place in seven days, that man descended from Adam and Eve and inherited from them a corrupt human nature, that a bloody sacrifice was needed to propitiate God and expiate man's sins, that Jesus' body rose from the tomb and that He will literally come again, but major voices are denying even that *God* is what theology traditionally said He was. For many who call themselves Christians, every item of every creed is subject to review, both because creeds are so patently products of the ages in which they were composed and were therefore subject to the scientific, philosophical, and religious understanding of bygone times, and because new knowledge and new ways of thinking enable the replacement of what seemed to be the metaphysical and religious requirements of an earlier day.

CHAPTER FOUR: *The Nature of Metaphysical Thinking*

1. Urban, *Language and Reality*, p. 181.

2. Whitehead, *Religion in the Making*, p. 130.

3. Langer, *Philosophy in a New Key*, p. 218.

4. Olford, "History, Theology, and Faith," *Theology Today*, XIV (April, 1957), 20.

5. Schilpp, "Is 'Standpointless Philosophy' Possible?" *Philosophical Review*, XLIV (May, 1935), 253.

6. Lovejoy, *The Great Chain of Being,* pp. 3–23.

7. Emmett, *The Nature of Metaphysical Thinking*, p. 12.

8. Tillich, *Systematic Theology*, I, 58.

9. Randall, "On Being Rejected," *Journal of Philosophy*, L (December 17, 1953, 798–99.

10. Hartshorne, *Reality as Social Process*, p. 175.

11. Emmett, *The Nature of Metaphysical Thinking*, p. v.

12. Pepper, "The Root Metaphor Theory of Metaphysics," *Journal of Philosophy*, XXXII (July 4, 1935), 369. The theory set forth here is expounded at greater length in *World Hypotheses* by the same author, but the original article is a marvelously comprehensive treatment.

13. Casserley, *The Christian in Philosophy*, pp. 224 and 226.

14. Whitehead, *Religion in the Making*, p. 84, *Science and the Modern World*, p. 158, and *Process and Reality*, p. 4, respectively. Hereafter these works will be abbreviated as RM, SMW, and PR respectively. *Adventures in Ideas* will be abbreviated as AI.

15. Pepper, "Metaphysical Method," *Philosophical Review*, LII (May, 1943), 252.

16. The latter part of the statement needs qualification. However, to have inserted the qualification in the text would have destroyed the literary effect. It is not clear that all simplifications are oversimplifications.

17. Dillenberger and Welch, *Protestant Christianity*, pp. 313–14.

18. Buber, *I and Thou*, p. 117.

19. Williams, "Theology and Truth," *Journal of Religion*, XXII (April, 1942), 392.

20. Langer, *Philosophy in a New Key*, p. 19.

21. Hampshire, "Metaphysical Systems," in Pears, ed., *The Nature of Metaphysics*, p. 31.

22. Hutchison, "The Religious Use of Language," *Christian Scholar*, XXXVIII (September, 1955), 183.

CHAPTER FIVE: *Symbols and Metaphysics*

1. Cassirer, *An Essay on Man*, p. 43.

2. Emmett, *The Nature of Metaphysical Thinking*, pp. 95, 60, 62, respectively.

3. Waismann, "Verifiability," in Flew, ed., *Logic and Language* (First Series), p. 141.

4. Wheelwright, *The Burning Fountain*, pp. 18–19.

5. Urban, *Language and Reality*, p. 470.

6. Urban, "Symbolism as a Theological Principle," *Journal of Religion*, XIX (1939), 21.

7. Farrar, *Finite and Infinite*, p. 2.

8. Moore's claim can be found in his *Principia Ethica*, a selection from which, entitled "The Indefinability of Good," is reprinted in *A Modern Introduction to Philosophy*, edited by Paul Edwards and Arthur Pap. Rudolph Otto speaks of "the holy" in a similar way in Chapters II–VII of *The Idea of the Holy*. Chapter VI of W. T. Stace's *Time and Eternity* sets forth most succinctly his views on mystical symbols.

9. Wieman, "Can God Be Perceived?" *Journal of Religion*, XXIII (January, 1943), 27.

10. Langer, *Philosophy in a New Key*, p. 55.

11. Whorf, *Collected Papers on Metalinguistics*, p. 5.

12. For a discussion of this doctrine the following sources are suggested. E. L. Mascall, *Existence and Analogy*, especially Chapter V, defends the principle. Dorothy Emmett, *The Nature of Metaphysical Thinking,* Chapter VII, attacks both the underlying proofs and the meaningfulness of this sort of analogy; Mascall's rejoinder to this attack is found in Chapter VII of the above book.

13. Langer, *Philosophy in a New Key*, p. 114.

14. This point has relevance to the discussion of this concept in Chapter Two. The point at issue there was whether or not Sidney Hook was correct in arguing that creation *ex nihilo* was logically meaningless because in human experience every instance of creation is one of creation from something.

15. Emmett. *The Nature of Metaphysical Thinking*, pp. 111 and 114.

16. Bevan, *Symbolism and Belief*, p. 336.

17. Dunbar, *Symbolism and Medieval Thought*, p. 7. This usage is endorsed by W. M. Urban in Chapter IX of *Language and Reality*.

18. Tillich, "The Religious Symbol," in May, ed., *Symbolism in*

Religion and Literature, p. 91; Wheelwright, *The Burning Fountain,* p. 288; and Urban, *Language and Reality,* p. 613.

CHAPTER SIX: *Problems Concerning Symbols of Transcendence*

1. Tillich, "Theology and Symbolism," in Johnson, ed., *Religious Symbolism,* p. 109.

2. *Ibid.,* pp. 111 and 113.

3. *Ibid.,* p. 111, and Tillich, *Theology of Culture,* pp. 65–66.

4. Tillich, *Theology of Culture,* p. 66.

5. Tillich, "Theology and Symbolism," p. 111.

6. Bevan, *Symbolism and Belief,* p. 339.

7. Calhoun, "How Shall We Think of God?" *Christendom,* I (1935–36), 609. This article is part of a lengthy exchange between Robert L. Calhoun and H. N. Wieman, Calhoun defending and Wieman rejecting the adequacy of personal categories.

8. Such a schema has been proposed by Frederick Sontag, "Perfection, Infinity and Univocity," *Review of Metaphysics,* VI (December, 1952), 219–32.

9. Tillich, *The Dynamics of Faith,* p. 52. This is also discussed at length in Tillich's *Systematic Theology,* I, 235 ff. J. N. Findlay makes basically the same point in arguing for the unreality of God. See his "Can God's Existence Be Disproved?" in Flew and MacIntyre, eds., *New Essays in Philosophical Theology.*

10. Mascall, *Existence and Analogy,* p. 95.

11. Stace, *Time and Eternity,* p. 95.

12. *Ibid.,* p. 150; see also pp. 59 and 74 for similar comments.

13. Charles Hartshorne makes the elaboration of this fundamental inconsistency in the classical tradition the central theme of his *The Divine Relativity.* It seems obvious to the present author that the question is proved; however, classicists seem to be remarkably unconcerned by it.

14. Stace, *Time and Eternity,* p. 91.

15. Emmett, *The Nature of Metaphysical Thinking,* p. 114. See also pp. 205 ff.

16. Buber, *I and Thou,* pp. 110–11. Theologians commonly object

to the use of "person" words for God. "Anthropomorphism" is a bad word. The reader might enjoy some other -isms and -olatries from the literature: mechanicomorphism, logicomorphism, ontolatry (worship of Being), etiolatry (worship of cause), and even *id*-olatry (worship of the vital or unconscious).

17. Buber, *Eclipse of God,* pp. 126–27.

18. Buber, *I and Thou,* p. 82.

19. Casserley, *The Christian in Philosophy,* p. 41.

20. Baillie, *God Was in Christ,* pp. 108–9.

21. Charles Hartshorne, *Beyond Humanism, Man's Vision of God, The Divine Relativity, Reality as Social Process,* and *The Logic of Perfection.*

22. Knudson, *Basic Issues in Christian Thought,* p. 74.

23. Katz, "Eternity—Shadow of Time," *Review of Religion,* XI (November, 1946), 40.

24. Bevan, *Symbolism and Belief,* p. 97.

25. Kierkegaard, *Concluding Unscientific Postscript,* pp. 107 and 170.

26. Tillich, *The Dynamics of Faith,* p. 49.

27. Bultmann, *Kergyma and Myth,* I, 10.

28. Casserley, "Event-Symbols and Myth-Symbols," *Anglican Theological Review,* XXXVIII (April, 1956), 133.

29. Cherbonnier, "Is There a Biblical Metaphysic?" *Theology Today,* XV (January, 1959), 458 and 459.

30. Cherbonnier, "Mystical vs. Biblical Symbolism," *The Christian Scholar,* XXXIX (March, 1958), 42.

31. Brunner, *Revelation and Reason,* p. 399.

32. Niebuhr, *The Meaning of Revelation,* p. 138.

33. Cherbonnier, "Is There a Biblical Metaphysic?" p. 466.

CHAPTER SEVEN: *Theism and Metaphysical Proof*

1. Hick, *Faith and Knowledge,* p. x. Hick argues that there is this internal coherence in Christian theism, that "if man is to be personal, God must be *deus absconditus.* He must, so to speak, stand back, hiding himself behind his creation, and leaving us the freedom

to recognize or fail to recognize his dealings with us" (p. 179). "In order to be cognitively free in relation to God we must possess an innate tendency to recognize his presence behind the phenomena of life, and yet a tendency which is not irresistible but which we may repress without doing manifest violence to our nature" (p. 184). Christianity, he argues, holds to the kind of God which such faith requires.

2. One highly unusual but perceptive form of this argument is that attributed to a Jew who, according to the story, reached Rome during the height of Papal corruption and who, on observing the Church, converted to Christianity. His reason, it is said, was that a Church so corrupt could have endured so long only if God supported it. There are prophetic voices in religion throughout the ages who would support this line of argument, that the only "proof" for God's existence is the fact that He has been able to maintain witness in His world despite the Church, or, more ecclesiastically put, that He has been able to keep His Church in existence despite the tendencies of the people who are in it.

3. Hick, *Faith and Knowledge*, p. 148.

4. Stace, *Religion and the Modern Mind*, p. 76.

CHAPTER EIGHT: *Metaphysics and Proof*

1. The seeming adequacy of a portion of a system can be undermined through the raising of such questions, thus pointing to the usefulness of isolating and questioning basic assumptions. Tillich's point that the God of personalistic theism must be surpassed because such a God is merely a being and not Being-itself seemed conclusive to the present author, until the question was raised as to whether or not there is such a thing as Being-itself. The hold of the assumption was broken. What seemed to be an indubitable point suddenly dissolved because it became clear that it was possible to doubt that Being is. Beings, yes—Being, no. A host of other examples could be provided, as ideas which seemed coercive have been successfully challenged.

2. Kaufman, *Relativism, Knowledge and Faith*, p. 116.

3. Kimpel, *Religious Faith, Language and Knowledge*, pp. 111–12.

Bibliography

Ayer, Alfred Jules. *Language, Truth, and Logic*. New York: Dover Publishers, n.d.

Baillie, D. M. *God Was in Christ*. New York: Charles Scribner's Sons, 1948.

Barth, Karl. *The Doctrine of the Word of God*. Part I. New York: Charles Scribner's Sons, 1936.

Bartsch, Hans Werner, ed. *Kerygma and Myth*. London: S.P.C.K., 1954.

Bevan, Edwyn. *Symbolism and Belief*. Boston. Beacon Press, 1957.

Brunner, Emil. *Revelation and Reason*. Philadelphia: Westminster Press, 1946.

Bryson, Lyman, and others, eds. *Symbols and Values: An Initial Study*. New York: Harper and Brothers, 1954.

Buber, Martin. *Eclipse of God*. New York: Harper and Brothers, 1952.

—— *I and Thou*. Edinburgh: T. & T. Clark, 1937.

Burtt, Edwin A. "The Status of 'World Hypotheses,'" *Philosophical Review*, LII (November, 1943), 590–601.

Calhoun, Robert L. "How Shall We Think of God?" *Christendom*, I (1935–36), 609.

Carnap, Rudolph. *Philosophy and Logical Syntax*. London: Kegan Paul, Trench, Trubner & Co., Ltd., 1935.

Casserley, J. V. Langmead. *The Christian in Philosophy*. New York: Charles Scribner's Sons, 1951.

—— "Event-Symbols and Myth-Symbols, I," *Anglican Theological Review*, XXXVIII (April, 1956), 127-37.

Cassirer, Ernst. *An Essay on Man*. Garden City, N.Y.: Doubleday & Company, Inc., 1953.

162   *Bibliography*

Cherbonnier, Edmond LaB. "Is There a Biblical Metaphysic?" *Theology Today*, XV (January, 1959), 454–69.

—— "Mystical vs. Biblical Symbolism," *Christian Scholar*, XXXIX (March, 1956), 32–44.

Come, Arnold B. "Theology Beyond Paradox," *Religion in Life*, XXV (Winter, 1955–56), 35–46.

Copleston, Frederick C. *Aquinas*. Baltimore: Penguin Books, Ltd., 1955.

—— "The Philosophical Relevance of Religious Experience," *Philosophy*, XXXI (July, 1956), 229–43.

Crombie, I. M. "The Possibility of Theological Statements," in Basil Mitchell, ed., *Faith and Logic*, pp. 31–83. London: George Allen & Unwin, Ltd., 1957.

—— "Theology and Falsification," in Antony Flew and Alasdair MacIntyre, eds., *New Essays in Philosophical Theology*, pp. 109–30. London: SCM Press, Ltd., 1955.

Dillenberger, John, and Claude Welch. *Protestant Christianity*. New York: Charles Scribner's Sons, 1954.

Dilley, Frank B. "Is There 'Knowledge' of God?" *Journal of Religion*, XXXVIII (April, 1958), 116–26.

Dunbar, Helen Flanders. *Symbolism in Medieval Thought*. New Haven: Yale University Press, 1929.

Edwards, Paul, and Arthur Pap. *A Modern Introduction to Philosophy*. New York: The Free Press of Glencoe, Inc., 1961.

Emmett, Dorothy. *The Nature of Metaphysical Thinking*. London: Macmillan and Co., Ltd., 1953.

Farrer, Austin. *Finite and Infinite*. Westminster: Dacre Press, 1943.

—— *The Glass of Vision*. Westminster: Dacre Press, 1948.

Feigl, Herbert. "Empiricism Versus Theology," in Paul Edwards and Arthur Pap, eds., *A Modern Introduction to Philosophy*, pp. 533–38. New York: The Free Press of Glencoe, Inc., 1961.

Ferré, Frederick. "Is Language About God Fraudulent?" *Scottish Journal of Theology*, XII (December, 1959), 337-60.

—— *Language, Logic and God*. New York: Harper and Brothers, 1961.

Findlay, J. N. "Can God's Existence Be Disproved?" in Antony Flew and Alasdair MacIntyre, eds., *New Essays in Philosophical Theology*, pp. 47–56. London: SCM Press, Ltd., 1955.

Flew, Antony. "Theology and Falsification," in Antony Flew and Alasdair MacIntyre, eds., *New Essays in Philosophical Theology*, pp. 96–99. London: SCM Press, Ltd., 1955.

Flew, Antony, ed. *Logic and Language*. First Series. New York: Philosophical Library, 1951.

Flew, Antony, and Alasdair MacIntyre, eds. *New Essays in Philosophical Theology*. London: SCM Press, Ltd., 1955.

Foster, Michael Beresford. *Mystery and Philosophy*. London: SCM Press, Ltd., 1957.

—— " 'We' in Modern Philosophy," in Basil Mitchell, ed., *Faith and Logic*, pp. 194–220. London: George Allen & Unwin, Ltd., 1957.

Hampshire, S. H. "Metaphysical Systems," in D. F. Pears, ed., *The Nature of Metaphysics*, pp. 23–38. London: Macmillan and Company, Ltd., 1957.

Hare, R. M. "Theology and Falsification," in Antony Flew and Alasdair MacIntyre, eds., *New Essays in Philosophical Theology*, pp. 99–103. London: SCM Press, Ltd., 1955.

Hartshorne, Charles. *Beyond Humanism*. Chicago: Willett, Clark & Company, 1937.

—— *The Divine Relativity*. New Haven: Yale University Press, 1948.

—— "The Idea of God—Literal or Analogical?" *Christian Scholar*, XXXIX (June, 1956), 131-36.

—— *The Logic of Perfection*. La Salle, Ill.: Open Court, 1962.

—— *Man's Vision of God and the Logic of Theism*. Chicago: Willett, Clark & Company, 1941.

—— *Reality as Social Process*. Glencoe, Ill.: The Free Press, 1953.

Hazelton, Roger. "The Nature of Christian Paradox," *Theology Today*, VI (October, 1949), 324–35.

Hepburn, Ronald W. *Christianity and Paradox*. London: Watts, 1958.

—— "Poetry and Religious Beliefs," in Alasdair MacIntyre, ed., *Metaphysical Beliefs*, pp. 85–166. London: SCM Press, Ltd., 1957.

Hick, John. *Faith and Knowledge*. Ithaca, N.Y.: Cornell University Press, 1957.

—— "God as Necessary Being," *Journal of Philosophy*, LVII (1960), 725–34.

Holmer, Paul. "The Nature of Religious Propositions," *Review of Religion*, XIX (March, 1955), 136–49.

Hook, Sidney. "Modern Knowledge and the Idea of God," *Commentary*, XXIX (1960), 207.

—— "Naturalism and Democracy," in Yervant H. Krikorian, ed., *Naturalism and the Human Spirit,* pp. 40-64. New York: Columbia University Press, 1944.

Hook, Sidney, ed. *Psychoanalysis, Scientific Method, and Philosophy.* New York: New York University Press, 1959.

Hutchinson, John A. *Faith, Reason and Existence.* New York: Oxford University Press, 1956.

—— "The Religious Use of Language," *Christian Scholar*, XXXVIII (September, 1955), 182–88.

Johnson, F. Ernest, ed. *Religious Symbolism.* New York: The Institute for Religious and Social Studies, 1955.

Jolivet, Regis. *The God of Reason.* London: Burns and Oates, 1959.

Katz, Joseph. "Eternity—Shadow of Time," *Review of Religion*, XI (November, 1946), 36–45.

Kaufman, Gordon D. *Relativism, Knowledge, and Faith.* Chicago: University of Chicago Press, 1960.

Kennick, William E. "The Language of Religion," *Philosophical Review*, LXV (January, 1956), 56–71.

—— "Metaphysical Presuppositions," *Journal of Philosophy*, LII (December 8, 1955), 769–80.

Kierkegaard, S. *Concluding Unscientific Postscript.* Princeton: Princeton University Press, 1944.

Kimpel, Ben. *Religious Faith, Language, and Knowledge.* New York: Philosophical Library, 1952.

Klemke, E. O. "Are Religious Statements Meaningful?" *Journal of Religion*, XL (January, 1960), 27–39.

Knudson, A. C. *Basic Issues in Christian Thought.* Nashville: Abingdon-Cokesbury Press, 1950.

Krikorian, Yervant H., ed. *Naturalism and the Human Spirit.* New York: Columbia University Press, 1944.

—— and Abraham Edel, eds. *Contemporary Philosophic Problems.* New York: The Macmillan Company, 1959.

Kroner, Richard. *How Do We Know God?* New York: Harper and Brothers, 1943.

Laird, John. *Recent Philosophy*. London: Oxford University Press, 1936.

Lamprecht, Sterling P. "Naturalism and Religion," in Yervant H. Krikorian, ed., *Naturalism and the Human Spirit*, pp. 17–39. New York: Columbia University Press, 1944.

Langer, Susanne. *Philosophy in a New Key*. New York: Mentor Books, 1948.

Lazerowitz, Morris. "The Relevance of Psychoanalysis to Philosophy," in Sidney Hook, ed., *Psychoanalysis, Scientific Method, and Philosophy*, pp. 133–56. New York: New York University Press, 1959.

—— *The Structure of Metaphysics*. London: Routledge & Kegan Paul, Ltd., 1955.

Lewis, H. D. "Contemporary Empiricism and the Philosophy of Religion," *Philosophy*, XXXII (July, 1957), 193–205.

Lovejoy, Arthur O. *The Great Chain of Being*. Cambridge, Mass.: Harvard University Press, 1936.

MacGregor, Geddes. "The Nature of Religious Utterance," *Christian Scholar*, XXXVIII (September, 1955), 173–81.

Machle, Edward J. "Symbols in Religion," *Journal of Bible and Religion*, XXI (July, 1953), 163–69.

Macintosh, D. C. "Is Theology Reducible to Mythology?" *Review of Religion*, IV (January, 1940), 140–58.

MacIntyre, Alasdair. "The Logical Status of Religious Belief," in Alasdair MacIntyre, ed., *Metaphysical Beliefs*, pp. 167–211. London: SCM Press, Ltd., 1957.

MacIntyre, Alasdair, ed. *Metaphysical Beliefs*. London: SCM Press, Ltd., 1957.

Margolis, Joseph. "What Is Religious Truth?" *Review of Religion*, XX (November, 1954), 38–46.

Martin, C. B. "A Religious Way of Knowing," in Antony Flew and Alasdair MacIntyre, eds., *New Essays in Philosophical Theology*, pp. 76–95. London: SCM Press, Ltd., 1955.

Martin, James Alfred, Jr. *Empirical Philosophies of Religion*. New York: King's Crown Press, 1945.

—— "Theology: Science or Art?" *Journal of Religion*, XXXII (January, 1952), 8–17.

Mascall, E. L. "The Doctrine of Analogy," *Cross Currents*, I (Summer, 1951), 38–57.

Mascall, E. L. *Existence and Analogy.* London: Longmans, Green and Co., 1949.

—— *He Who Is.* London: Longmans, Green and Co., 1943.

May, Rollo, ed. *Symbolism in Religion and Literature.* New York: George Braziller, 1960.

Meland, Bernard. "Interpreting the Christian Faith Within a Philosophical Perspective," *Journal of Religion,* XXXIII (April, 1953), 87–102.

—— "Theological Perspectives," *Religion in Life,* XIII (Winter, 1943–44), 100–106.

Mitchell, Basil, ed. *Faith and Logic.* London: George Allen & Unwin, Ltd., 1957.

Nagel, Ernest. "Naturalism Reconsidered," in Yervant H. Krikorian and Abraham Edel, eds., *Contemporary Philosophic Problems,* pp. 337–49. New York: The Macmillan Company, 1959.

Niebuhr, H. Richard. *The Meaning of Revelation.* New York: The Macmillan Company, 1941.

Olford, John E. "History, Theology, and Faith," *Theology Today,* XIV (April, 1957), 15–28.

Ostow, Mortimer, and Ben-Ami Scharfstein. *The Need to Believe.* New York: International University Press, Inc., 1954.

Otis, Brooks. "Mythos and Logos," *Christian Scholar,* XXXIII (September, 1955), 219–31.

Pears, D. F., ed. *The Nature of Metaphysics.* London: Macmillan and Company, Ltd., 1957.

Pepper, Stephen. "Metaphysical Method," *Philosophical Review,* LII (May, 1943), 252–69.

—— "The Root-Metaphor Theory of Metaphysics," *Journal of Philosophy,* XXXII (July 4, 1935), 365–74.

—— *World Hypotheses.* Berkeley, Calif.: University of California Press, 1942.

Popkin, Richard H. "Theological and Religious Scepticism," *Christian Scholar,* XXXIX (June, 1956), 150–58.

Ramsey, Ian T. *Religious Language: An Empirical Placing of Theological Phrases.* London: SCM Press, Ltd., 1957.

Randall, John Herman, Jr. "On Being Rejected," *Journal of Philosophy,* L (December 17, 1953), 797–805.

—— "Symposium: Are Religious Dogmas Cognitive and Meaningful," *Journal of Philosophy*, LI (March 4, 1954), 158–63.

Russell, Bertrand. *Why I Am Not a Christian*. New York: Simon and Schuster, 1963.

Schilpp, Paul A. "Is 'Standpointless Philosophy' Possible?" *Philosophical Review*, XLIV (May, 1935), 227–53.

Schlick, Moritz. "Meaning and Verification," *Philosophical Review*, XLV (July, 1936), 339–69.

Sittler, Joseph. "The Necessity of Faith," *Christian Scholar*, XXXVIII (September, 1955), 198–205.

Smart, Ninian. *Reasons and Faiths*. New York: Humanities Press, 1959.

Smith, Huston. "The Operational View of God: A Study of the Impact of Metaphysics on Religious Thought," *Journal of Religion*, XXXI (April, 1951), 94–113.

Sontag, Frederick. "Perfection, Infinity and Univocity," *Review of Metaphysics*, VI (December, 1952), 219–32.

Stace, W. T. *Religion and the Modern Mind*. Philadelphia: J. P. Lippincott Company, 1952.

—— *Time and Eternity*. Princeton: Princeton University Press, 1952.

Taubes, Jacob. "Dialectic and Analogy," *Journal of Religion*, XXXIV (April, 1954), 111–19.

Thomas, George. "Myth and Symbol in Religion." *Journal of Bible and Religion*, VII (November, 1939), 163–71.

Thompson, Samuel. "Philosophy and Theology: A Reply to Professor W. F. Zuurdeeg," *Journal of Religion*, XL (January, 1960), 9–17.

Tillich, Paul. *The Dynamics of Faith*. New York: Harper and Brothers, 1957.

—— "The Religious Symbol," in Rollo May, ed., *Symbolism in Religion and Literature*, pp. 75–98. New York: George Braziller, 1960.

—— *Systematic Theology*. Vol I. Chicago: University of Chicago Press, 1951.

—— "Theology and Symbolism," in F. Ernest Johnson, ed., *Religious Symbolism*, pp. 107–16. New York: The Institute for Religious and Social Studies, 1955.

—— *Theology of Culture*. New York: Oxford University Press, 1959.

Urban, Wilbur Marshall. *Language and Reality*. London: George Allen & Unwin, Ltd., 1939.

—— "Symbolism as a Theological Principle," *Journal of Religion*, XIX (January, 1939), 1–32.

Waismann, Friedrich. "Verifiability," in Antony Flew, ed., *Logic and Language*. First Series. Pp. 117-44. New York: Philosophical Library, 1951.

Wheelwright, Philip. *The Burning Fountain*. Bloomington, Ind.: Indiana University Press, 1954.

Whitehead, Alfred North. *Adventures in Ideas*. New York: Mentor Books, 1955.

—— *Process and Reality*. Humanities Press Edition. New York: The Macmillan Company, 1929.

—— *Religion in the Making*. New York: The Macmillan Company, 1926.

—— *Science and the Modern World*. New York: Mentor Books, 1948.

Whorf, Benjamin Lee. *Collected Papers on Metalinguistics*. Washington, D.C.: Foreign Service Institute, 1952.

Wieman, Henry Nelson. "Can God Be Perceived?" *Journal of Religion*, XXIII (January, 1943), 23–32.

Williams, Daniel Day. "Theology and Truth," *Journal of Religion*, XXII (April, 1942), 382–97.

—— "Truth in the Theological Perspective," *Journal of Religion*, XXVIII (October, 1948), 242–54.

Wisdom, John, "Gods," in Antony Flew, ed., *Logic and Language*. First Series. Pp. 187–206. New York: Philosophical Library, 1951.

Zuurdeeg, Willem F. *An Analytical Philosophy of Religion*. New York: Abingdon Press, 1958.

Index